THE GREAT LIVES SERIES

Great Lives biographies shed an exciting new light on the many dynamic men and women whose actions, visions, and dedication to an ideal have influenced the course of history. Their ambitions, dreams, successes and failures, the controversies they faced and the obstacles they overcame are the true stories behind these distinguished world leaders, explorers, and great Americans.

Other biographies in the Great Lives Series

A special thanks to educators Dr. Frank Moretti, Ph.D., Associate Headmaster of the Dalton School in New York City; Dr. Paul Mattingly, Ph.D., Professor of History at New York University; and Barbara Smith, M.S., Assistant Superintendent of the Los Angeles Unified School District, for their contributions to the Great Lives Series.

THOMAS JEFFERSON
The Philosopher President

John W. Selfridge

FAWCETT COLUMBINE
NEW YORK

For middle-school readers

A Fawcett Columbine Book
Published by Ballantine Books

Library of Congress Catalog Card Number: 90-92954

ISBN: 0-449-90379-6

Cover design and illustration by Paul Davis Studio

Manufactured in the United States of America

First Edition: November 1991

10 9 8 7 6 5 4 3 2 1

TABLE OF CONTENTS

THOMAS JEFFERSON

Jefferson Memorial, Washington D.C.

1

Freedom Writer

IN JUNE 1776, a robust young planter from Virginia named Thomas Jefferson sat alone in a simply furnished room on the second floor of a boarding house. He had taken up lodging in a small brick building on Market Street in Philadelphia, because it offered quiet surroundings and an absence of distractions. The job he had to do required the utmost concentration.

He placed a portable mahogany writing box—one that he designed and that was built especially for him by a Philadelphia cabinetmaker—securely on his lap. Then he carefully dipped his pen into the inkwell. He found it very difficult to begin. His eyes wandered from the page, and he gazed out the open window. The summer sun was pouring into the room, filling it with light and stifling heat. He looked at the coarse parchment in front of him and breathed deeply. He was perspiring and had a pounding headache. He put down his pen, reached for his handkerchief, and wiped his forehead.

For a moment he dwelled on the memory of his mother, who had died only three months before, and he worried about his wife, who was sick in bed back home in Virginia. Then as the sun slowly set, his mind returned to the task at hand. He began to think about the age-old conflict between freedom and government, made notes, and began to write.

Thomas Jefferson's assignment was an enormous one—to produce "an expression of the American mind" that would chart the course of history. Revolution was in the air, and this document had to convey the great urgency of that particular moment in America's history.

When the Continental Congress had met earlier that month, there was considerable discussion about independence for Britain's American colonies. Delegates from New York, New Jersey, Pennsylvania, and South Carolina were opposed to severing colonial ties. With such mixed feelings among the delegates, the Congress appointed a committee to explore the matter more fully and to draft a statement that would declare the reasons for severing those ties.

Five delegates were chosen for the committee: Benjamin Franklin of Pennsylvania, John Adams of Massachusetts, Thomas Jefferson of Virginia, Roger Sherman of Connecticut, and Robert Livingston of New York. Thomas Jefferson, a wealthy young planter, was asked by his fellow committee members to write the first draft of the declaration. Hesitating to take on the huge responsibility, Jefferson tried unsuccessfully to convince his colleague John Adams from Massachusetts to write it. Forty-six years later Adams recalled his conversation with Jefferson.

"Why will you not? You ought to do it," Jefferson urged his highly esteemed colleague.

"Reasons enough," Adams replied.

"What can be your reasons?" asked Jefferson.

"Reason first," Adams answered, "You are a Virginian, and a Virginian ought to appear at the head of this business. Reason second, I am obnoxious, suspected, and unpopular. You are very much otherwise. Reason third, you can write ten times better than I can."

"Well," conceded Jefferson, seeing that he would not be able to change Adams's mind, "If you are decided, I will do as well as I can."

Jefferson had to write a declaration that would embody the spirit of America—one that would assert the basic rights of individuals and peoples, justify a revolution, and inspire the people to bring it about. It had to proclaim lofty principles such as freedom, equality, justice, and democracy; but it also had to be written in a concise, logical manner that would appeal to common sense and be understood by all those who read it or heard it read.

A leading spokesman in the movement for American independence, Thomas Jefferson put his heart, mind, and soul to the task. He had already earned a reputation for being an excellent writer and an extremely knowledgeable scholar and lawyer. He drew on his extensive background in history, philosophy, and literature, and on his knowledge of the works of many of the great political thinkers, such as John Locke, Thomas Reid, George Mason, and Thomas Paine.

Jefferson was not trying to create an original piece of writing in which to break new intellectual ground.

3

Rather, he was striving to articulate in the best language possible the sentiments of his countrymen. The angry American people were fed up with the British monarch and long frustrated by their futile attempts to be heard in the faraway Parliament in London, England. They were ready to rise up in revolt.

Gradually words became phrases, which in turn became sentences. In his quiet Philadelphia boarding house Jefferson wrote, edited, scratched out, and rewrote until his hand ached and his vision became blurry. Finally the elegant yet powerful Declaration of Independence began to take shape under Jefferson's pen.

"When in the Course of human events, it becomes necessary for one people to dissolve the political bands which have connected them with another, and to assume among the powers of the earth, the separate and equal station to which the Laws of Nature and of Nature's God entitle them . . ."

"We hold these truths to be sacred and undeniable," he wrote. Then he quickly crossed out "sacred and undeniable," replaced the phrase with the words "self-evident," and continued. "We hold these truths to be self-evident, that all men are created equal, that they are endowed by their Creator with certain unalienable Rights, that among these are Life, Liberty, and the pursuit of Happiness."

Jefferson stated that when these essential rights are infringed upon by an exceedingly oppressive government, entirely insensitive to the needs and rights of citizens, the people had a right to break all political ties with that government.

The document Jefferson wrote called for a rebellion against British colonial rule and the establishment of a new, independent nation. Touching on popular grievances from all corners of America, he listed numerous acts of tyranny that the British monarch, George III, had committed. He denounced the king for quartering British troops in the colonies without the consent of their legislatures, for forcing Americans to pay for the British soldiers' food and shelter, for imposing heavy taxes on the colonies without their having representation in the British Parliament, and for some two dozen other acts of oppression. To denounce the British king was a serious matter—in fact, a blatant act of treason, punishable by death—but Jefferson also knew that the time for caution was past, and the time for American independence had come.

Fearlessly he declared the colonies to be free and independent states, no longer with any political ties to the British Crown. Finally, with full knowledge of the many sacrifices that would be demanded of his fellow Americans to further the revolutionary cause, Jefferson wrote, "And for the support of this Declaration, we mutually pledge to each other our lives, our fortunes, and our sacred honor."

Jefferson delivered copies of the Declaration to Adams and Franklin, who made various suggestions for improving it by writing notes in the margins and editing the text. After considering the comments of his fellow committee members, Jefferson submitted the Declaration for the Continental Congress's approval. Representatives from throughout the colonies came to Philadelphia to read, analyze, and discuss the document; to suggest improvements; and ultimately to cast their vote for or against it.

In July, after many long hours of vigorous, sometimes bitter debate and painstaking revision, two colonies—South Carolina and Pennsylvania—remained opposed to a Congressional motion for independence, while New York and Delaware were undecided. By the end of the second day of heated debate, only New York was uncommitted. While New York leaders debated among themselves, 12 of the 13 colonies took a vote. The Continental Congress approved the Declaration of Independence on July 4, 1776.

The preparation of a printed copy of the document on heavy parchment was then ordered, and a meeting for a formal signing of the Declaration by the delegates to the Congress was scheduled. While the copy was being printed, the text of the Declaration was read aloud in the yard of the Philadelphia State House on July 8.

A crowd of anxious and concerned citizens gathered to listen. At times during the reading they were silent, listening carefully to every word. At other times there were outbursts of cheers. When the reading was over, the crowd's reaction was joyous. The spirit of revolution spread quickly throughout the colonies.

The formal signing of the Declaration took place in Philadelphia on August 2, 1776. Signing the document was an act of treason punishable with death by hanging, so it was carried out behind closed doors. As a result, few people other than members of the Continental Congress knew that Jefferson was the author of the Declaration. It was not until later that Jefferson received credit for writing it. Also, because of the secrecy, numerous stories became common throughout the colonies.

One such tale involved the enormously fat and

good-humored Philadelphia physician Benjamin Rush, who upon signing the Declaration reportedly turned to the especially thin Elbridge Gerry, a delegate from Massachusetts. Said Rush, "I shall have a great advantage over you, Mr. Gerry, when we are all hung [sic] for what we are now doing. From the size and weight of my body I shall die in a few minutes, but from the lightness of your body, you will dance in the air an hour or two before you are dead."

Rush's comment was only partly in jest. The revolution had yet to be fought, and there was no guarantee the struggle against the British would succeed. There was real reason for the Congressional delegates to fear for their lives.

As news of the Declaration spread to American cities and towns, debtors, who were considered victims of outrageous taxation, were released from prison. George III was burned, ridiculed, or buried in effigy in public squares. The anthem "God Save the King" was left out of morning and evening church services. Signs bearing the royal coat of arms were torn down and often burned ceremoniously before crowds of people. The text of the Declaration was printed on handbills and distributed among the colonial armed forces.

General George Washington ordered the Declaration read aloud to his troops, hoping they would be inspired by its rousing tone. John Adams wrote of the Declaration, "It compleats a Revolution, which will make as good a Figure in the History of Mankind, as any that has preceded it . . . . All America is remarkably united."

As enthusiastic as Adams was, in 1776 neither he, Jefferson, nor any of their friends could have foreseen

Young Thomas Jefferson reading a draft of the Declaration of Independence to Benjamin Franklin in Philadelphia, June, 1776. Jefferson and Franklin were part of a committee appointed by the Continental Congress to write a statement setting out the reasons for declaring independence from Great Britain. Doing so was considered an act of treason, and they faced the hangman if they failed.

that the Declaration of Independence would be cherished by generations of Americans to come. The Declaration of Independence became a priceless national treasure, not only for its historical value with respect to the founding of the United States of America, but for its universal themes of freedom, equality, justice, and democracy. These ideals are at the foundation of American society and government, and have inspired democratic movements around the world for more than two centuries.

2

The Stirrings of Youth

THOMAS JEFFERSON WAS born on April 13, 1743, on a Virginia tobacco plantation called Shadwell, located on the fertile banks of the Rivanna River in Albemarle County. Growing up, he came to know the pungent smell of drying tobacco plants, the haze that lay over the rolling land on a hot summer morning. He listened to the distant voices of his father's slaves, who sometimes sang languorous melodies as they worked the fields, their black bodies glistening with sweat under the hot southern sun.

Thomas Jefferson's father, Peter Jefferson, was a surveyor and mapmaker. His mother, Jane Randolph, was the daughter of a wealthy James River landowner. Though Peter Jefferson had very little formal education, he had a keen, natural intelligence and an intense eagerness to learn. He taught himself a trade and eventually became a successful and highly respected member of his community. As he accumulated wealth, land—and black slaves—he also became one of Virginia's leading tobacco growers. He was known as a prosperous and greatly admired businessman. Much later in his life Thomas Jefferson wrote, "My father's education had been quite neglected; but being of a strong mind, sound judgment and eager after information, he read much and improved himself."

At a very early age Thomas Jefferson showed that he had inherited his father's intelligence, ingenuity, and will to learn. Peter Jefferson made sure his son had every opportunity to get the best education money could buy. At first Thomas studied with private tutors. When the boy was old enough, his father sent him to boarding school in Fredericksville, a little more than 10 miles from Shadwell, to study the classics. Thomas soon proved to be an excellent student, but Peter Jefferson never lived to witness his son's academic achievements. He died in August 1757, when Thomas was only 14.

The Fredericksville Parish and School was a modest log schoolhouse run by an Anglican pastor named James Maury, a man known throughout the colonies for his great learning. Thomas enjoyed the academic environment at Fredericksville, and he excelled in every subject. He studied not only the required classical languages, Latin and Greek, but he read the great works of world literature as well. He took a particular liking to the French dramatist Molière and the Spanish writer Cervantes, author of *Don Quixote.* He also studied the Gaelic language and European history, which became one of his favorite subjects in school.

In addition to these academic pursuits, the young

Jefferson studied dancing and the violin with private teachers. Each day Jefferson attended his classes, did his homework, and spent hours reading books in the school's excellent library. Learning truly excited him, and this excitement would last all his life.

When he was about to turn 17 years old, Jefferson enrolled in the College of William and Mary in Williamsburg, Virginia. Williamsburg was a prosperous town and the home of many of the most celebrated people in the American colonies. Many lawyers, doctors, and politicians resided there with their families in elegant red brick houses.

The bustling Virginia town offered great prosperity for the merchants and tradesmen who conducted business there. Shop windows displayed fine items, often imported from Europe, and well-heeled citizens traveled through the town in shiny wooden horse-drawn carriages. The town of Williamsburg brought the senses to life. Walking down its cobblestone streets, one might catch the smell of a hearty roast through the window of a crowded tavern and hear the lively roar of conversation even above the clip-clop and rumble of a passing delivery cart or the chatter of friendly townspeople. When Thomas Jefferson arrived in Williamsburg, well-read yet an innocent country boy from the Albemarle hills, he was overwhelmed by the small yet cosmopolitan city.

Because he had worked hard in the demanding academic program at Reverend Maury's school, Jefferson had advanced well beyond even the best students at William and Mary. He soon found himself unchallenged and frustrated. Luckily, Doctor William Small, a professor of mathematics and natural philosophy at the college, noticed Jefferson was unhappy and decided to do something about it. He introduced the young man to the prominent lawyer George Wythe and the economist Francis Fauquier, who was lieutenant governor of Virginia. These three men—Small, Wythe, and Fauquier—inspired Jefferson with their knowledge of history, politics, law, and philosophy. They frequently invited the young man into a local tavern and engaged him in conversation over a pint of ale or a glass of port. Their wide-ranging discussions opened the young man's mind to a wealth of knowledge and the many possibilities life has to offer.

Still, Jefferson was not so distracted by ale and conversation that he neglected his school books. In fact he was becoming an ever more serious student under the guidance of Small and his colleagues. Jefferson left William and Mary after two years of study, and in 1762, after much agonizing over the decision, Jefferson decided he would become a lawyer.

Since he had inherited land and money from his father, Jefferson did not seek to practice law simply for the generous fees he could earn. He believed that by acquiring a broad knowledge of the law he would be better prepared to work for the betterment of society. Men who were familiar with the workings of law, business, and government had many opportunities available to them.

Today in the United States law students enroll at a university in a program that consists of at least three years of intensive study. Their studies are very demanding, and once someone has earned a degree from an accredited law school, he or she must still pass a tough written examination administered by the state before actually practicing law.

In Jefferson's day there was no such thing as a law school and no program of required courses to follow. There were a number of books that were recommended for students of the law, mostly English essays such as Lord Kame's "Historical Law Tracts." Generally one studied the law just as one prepared to become a blacksmith or a candlemaker—by becoming an apprentice.

Jefferson apprenticed to his college mentor, the lawyer George Wythe. For five years he observed and took notes on Wythe's every move in court, at the office, and at business meetings. In so doing, Jefferson met many other lawyers, some of them extremely influential and highly respected, and he learned by watching them closely as well. Before long Jefferson had begun to acquire substantial knowledge of the law.

Jefferson was able to find time to tend to the family plantation at Shadwell when not assisting Wythe. Though Jefferson very often spent long days reading and taking notes, he frequently stole a moment to escape to the outdoors and lose himself in the natural splendor of the lush Virginia countryside. He enjoyed hiking on the footpaths of the Albemarle hills and riding horses along their many winding trails. Reading also continued to be his passion.

As time passed, Jefferson grew into a strikingly handsome young man. He stood more than 6 feet tall at a time when the average man was only 5 feet, 6 inches. He had thick, reddish hair that he brushed back from his forehead; gray eyes flecked with hazel; a sturdy, wiry build; and strong, distinguished facial features. He carried himself loosely, and often seemed physically awkward and undignified to some people.

Although fairly reserved and soft-spoken, Jefferson was by no means somber. His charm and ease in conversation made him very engaging, even magnetic, in social settings. But his calm exterior was quite different from the rather intense, emotional convictions that characterized his inner life.

As a young man, Jefferson had a very active interest in women, and they in him. His relationships, though, were either friendly or mere passing fancies—until he met Rebecca Burwell. Jefferson was attracted to her the moment they met at a ball in the Apollo Room of Raleigh's Tavern in 1762. She was only 16 years old, but women married young in Jefferson's day. Unfortunately for Jefferson, Rebecca Burwell did not return the affection he lavished on her. In fact she decided to marry someone else. When Jefferson heard of her engagement to another, he was crushed. He resolved never to allow himself to become infatuated with a woman again.

Jefferson was admitted to the Virginia bar in 1767 and began practicing law. He argued many difficult cases, mostly involving disputes over real estate. These cases usually demanded extensive preparation, and scheduled court appearances often required long journeys on horseback to get to the courthouse. At first Jefferson found the practice of law to be a difficult challenge, but he worked hard and soon began to reap the many rewards of the profession. Before long he had established a successful law practice and a wide reputation for professional excellence.

Despite the demands of legal work Jefferson continued to oversee the Shadwell plantation, a full-time job even with the large number of slaves Jefferson had to perform the manual labor. With his characteristic diligence he was able to sustain a busy and successful law practice and still keep Shadwell productive.

While Jefferson, planter and lawyer, was engaged in the pursuit of two careers, the political climate in America was becoming increasingly volatile. Relations between the colonies and Great Britain had been cooperative and even cordial until 1763, when Britain emerged victorious over France in the French and Indian Wars, a nine-year struggle for control of the North American continent. Until that point both France and England had had military, economic, and political interests in America. With the British victory, the French had very little remaining influence. England's control of the American colonies, however, did not come without cost. The victory left Britain with a huge national debt and the enormous burden of maintaining its vast new territorial possession both administratively and militarily. England attempted to force the colonies, through the imposition of heavy taxes, to pay a large share of the cost of maintaining the empire.

A series of administrative measures strained relations between Britain and its North American colonies. In 1764 the British Parliament passed the Sugar Act, which raised duties on sugar, coffee, and imports entering the colonies from the West Indies. The Sugar Act also placed severe restrictions on colonial trade and provided for strict customs enforcement. Then the English Parliament passed the Currency Act, a measure that outlawed the printing of currency in the colonies, allowing only British currency to be used as money. In 1765 Parliament passed the Quartering Act, a law requiring the colonists to provide comfortable lodging, candles, food, and drink for British soldiers, free of charge and on demand. Also that year Parliament passed the Stamp Act, a law requiring colonists to buy only British paper that bore an official tax stamp. Colonists were outraged by these moves. For many, the Stamp Act was the last straw.

The voice of protest was raised throughout the colonies, and rebellion became the order of the day. In Boston, the Sons of Liberty, a radical political group bent on freeing the colonies from British rule and led by Samuel Adams, encouraged and enforced resistance to the Stamp Act. On August 26, 1765, a mob brandishing sticks and rocks raided the house of Andrew Oliver, the British government official who had sponsored the Stamp Act. Colonists then boycotted British goods, bringing many businesses to a halt. Mass actions—in the form of boycotts, demonstrations, and even armed insurrections aimed at specific political goals—swept the colonies.

Perhaps the strongest and most persuasive voice of protest was that of the lawyer Patrick Henry. Jefferson had admired Henry for years and was a guest at a session of the Virginia legislature, or House of Burgesses in 1765 when Henry attacked British colonial policies and vowed outright resistance. "If this be treason," Henry declared, "make the most of it."

Just as the British colonies were on the verge of revolt, William Pitt, the new British prime minister, denounced the Stamp Act as "the most impolitic, arbitrary, oppressive, and unconstitutional act that ever was passed." Soon after it was repealed.

The British Parliament, however, still with no solution to its financial problems, resumed its effort to impose heavy taxes on the colonies despite the resistance. In 1767 Parliament passed the Townshend Acts, which levied taxes on paper, ink, tea, and glass. Once more the colonists were provoked and angry.

While tensions between England and America grew, Jefferson, now in his mid-20s, was establishing a reputation as a fine lawyer and a budding politician. In 1769 he was elected to the Virginia House of Burgesses. The following year that body adopted resolutions challenging the British Parliament's right to levy taxes in the colonies. Members of the House of Burgesses argued that because the colonies were not represented in the British Parliament in London, the British government's tax policies in the colonies were unjustified. They claimed that taxation without representation was unfair.

In response to this argument, the colonial governor of Virginia dissolved the House of Burgesses. Meeting informally in the Apollo Room of the Raleigh Tavern in Williamsburg, the legislators pledged to boycott all goods on which England levied taxes, until the Townshend Acts were repealed.

The boycott decision along with continued British oppression set off another wave of violent confrontations throughout the colonies. Colonists were outraged by the treatment they were receiving from the British. Since they had no representation in the British Parliament, more and more American colonists felt they had no alternative but to take up arms and rebel.

One act of rebellion became known as the 1770 Boston Massacre. On March 5, a group of colonists provoked British soldiers on duty there, and a riot resulted. The troops fired their weapons, and five American colonists were killed, including Crispus Attucks, a black man and the group's leader. Many others were wounded.

In the midst of this turmoil, Jefferson was devastated by a personal tragedy. In February 1770, a fire at Shadwell virtually destroyed his house and its contents, including his valuable library. Rather than dwell on the loss, however, Jefferson immediately set about building a new home. He selected the perfect spot, just across the Rivanna River from Shadwell, overlooking Albemarle County's lovely rolling hills. He named the place Monticello, Italian for "little mountain."

And what a house it would be! Jefferson immersed himself totally in the project, one that would occupy him for the next 40 years. It would result in one of the most splendid estates anywhere in America. In many ways, Monticello was an extension of Jefferson himself—it was a work of art that embodied his character and interests. Eventually the mansion contained Jefferson's vast library, his many inventions, and his personal art collection. It was there that he wrote numerous articles and essays and received important visitors. The grounds of the estate reflected Jefferson's love for planting and landscaping.

With his new house gradually becoming a home, by the age of twenty-eight Thomas Jefferson yearned for the company of a woman. Though he had sworn himself to bachelorhood following his ill-fated romance with Rebecca Burwell, he had a dramatic change of heart in 1770 when he met a 23-year-old widow named Martha Wayles Skelton. A bright, attractive heiress to a sizeable fortune, Skelton might have turned any committed bachelor into an eligible suitor. She was extremely poised and very well educated. The product of a cultured upbringing, she loved to dance and sing, and she played the harpsichord and spinet. During their courtship, Martha and Thomas played duets together, Thomas struggling at the violin to match her keyboard skills. Martha Skelton, a striking beauty with large brown eyes and dark red hair, was an obvious complement to Jefferson's rugged features and strong presence. Moreover, she was experienced in domestic matters, including keeping a household budget and overseeing servants.

On December 3, 1771, Jefferson applied for a marriage license, and on January 1, 1772, the two were married in a small but splendid ceremony.

The newlyweds spent their honeymoon at Monticello, braving a severe snowstorm to get there. In September they were blessed with a baby girl, whom they named Martha. Though she was a delicate baby, little Martha gained strength each day and gradually took on a healthy Jeffersonian glow. A second daughter was born to the couple in 1774. Extremely frail as an infant, she died the following year.

In subsequent years Martha Jefferson gave birth to six children, but only daughters: Martha, whom they called Patsy, and Mary, whom they called Polly and later Maria, survived infancy. Martha Jefferson's son John, from her previous marriage, died in early childhood the summer before she married Thomas. Despite the grief they felt at losing so many children, Thomas and Martha Jefferson were grateful for their blessings, loved each other very much, and lived happily together.

While Jefferson was enjoying his new life as a husband and father, the British Parliament passed the Tea Act in the spring of 1773. This legislation allowed an important British tea importer, the East India Company, to sell its tea in the colonies at lower prices than the Dutch tea most Americans drank.

The Tea Act was a Parliamentary effort to bail out the East India Company, which was financially troubled. Parliament's strategy, in addition to saving the British firm, was to get the colonists to buy British tea. The Act also imposed a revenue duty on all tea sold in the colonies. Again the colonists were outraged and began to prepare for an armed resistance.

In retaliation against the British, on the night of December 16, 1773, a group of colonists dressed in headdresses and other American Indian clothing boarded three English ships in Boston Harbor and heaved the ships' cargo, mostly cartons of tea, overboard. The Boston Tea Party, as this bold act of rebellion came to be known, prompted the British Parliament in 1774 to pass what the colonists called the Intolerable Acts. This legislation closed Boston Harbor and strengthened the British military presence in the colonies.

Jefferson and other colonial leaders felt that the colonists must be ruled only by laws they passed in their own legislative assemblies. In 1774, Jefferson presented his views in a political pamphlet which came to be called *A Summary View of the Rights of British America.* The work established him as one of America's most influential writers and political thinkers. In the *Summary* Jefferson argued that people were endowed with certain basic freedoms that could not rightly be denied by government. Among these, he wrote, was the right to self-determination—

the right for people to determine their own form of government and the future of their country.

The political tension in the colonies was at the breaking point, and Jefferson concluded that independence from British rule was the clearest solution. In the *Summary* Jefferson did not call for freedom from the British at all costs, as he would later, but he did challenge the authority of the British Parliament in America. Though many American leaders, including Jefferson's mentor George Wythe, urged caution and hoped the colonies' disputes with England could be resolved, Jefferson did not think that was possible.

On September 5, 1774, the First Continental Congress convened in Philadelphia. Delegates from all the colonies except Georgia were in attendance. They demanded that England repeal all objectionable laws passed since 1763, and they issued a proclamation asserting the colonies' right to tax their own people, the right of colonists to choose their own political representatives, and the right to have all foreign armies removed from colonial soil. The delegates officially encouraged civil disobedience and vowed to boycott British goods if their demands were not met. They also formed what was called the Continental Association to enforce the general boycott.

Meanwhile in Massachusetts, companies of "minutemen"—as the colonial troops were called because of their willingness to bear arms at a minute's notice—were forming and preparing for armed revolt against the British.

In the spring of 1775 the British monarch, George III, decided that military force was necessary to put down the upstart colonists. He believed they posed a real threat to British rule in America. But the colonists were now a unified freedom movement. Though they were not as well equipped for an armed struggle as the British were, they were ready to make great sacrifices to gain their freedom. King George knew that the independence movement had to be stopped quickly if the colonies were to remain under British control.

On the night of April 18 a gallant horseman named Paul Revere spread the word that the British were planning an attack. As he rode through the black night, he cried, "The British are coming! The British are coming!" stirring families from their sleep. The following day more than 1,000 British soldiers left Boston on a mission to destroy the munitions arsenal the colonists had gathered at Concord, Massachusetts. Thanks to Revere, the colonial Minutemen were ready. They surprised the British soldiers at Lexington. When the smoke cleared from the famous "shots heard 'round the world," eight Americans were dead and another ten were wounded.

The English troops marched to Concord and destroyed the arsenal, but they suffered 273 dead and wounded. This had been the first battle of the American Revolution. All out war seemed inevitable.

That year, Jefferson, now 32 years old, served as a delegate to the Continental Congress. The brightest and most powerful men in the colonies were members. The oldest member, Benjamin Franklin from Philadelphia, was known throughout the colonies as a great diplomat, writer, and inventor. Cousins John and Samuel Adams of Massachusetts, the lawyer John Jay of New York, the politician and writer John Dickinson of Pennsylvania; all these men were extremely well educated and widely recognized throughout the colonies for their accomplishments.

That summer the British engaged the Americans at the bloody Battle of Bunker Hill on the Charlestown peninsula outside of Boston. Both sides suffered heavy casualties. As the inevitability of a full-scale war with England became apparent, the Continental Congress took steps to prepare for battle. One of the first matters at hand was the formation of an army. General George Washington was appointed commander of the Continental Army, and efforts were made to raise money to fund a war with England.

Jefferson was asked by Congress to draft a paper explaining the colonies' reasons for taking up arms against the British. After a Congressional committee reviewed it, the paper was revised by John Dickinson. He toned down some of Jefferson's fiery language, which the committee found too radical. Entitled *Declaration of the Cause and Necessity for Taking Up Arms,* the paper contained the seeds of many of the ideas Jefferson would develop later in the Declaration of Independence.

Jefferson returned to Monticello during the Christmas season, 1775, to find his wife in ill health. For several months he remained at Monticello helping Martha along the road to recovery. Then his mother became ill. Martha's condition slowly improved, but Jefferson's mother died.

While he was at Monticello in March 1776, mourning his mother's death, Jefferson read a political pamphlet entitled *Common Sense* that had recently been published and distributed in the colonies. Its author, the radical Thomas Paine, was a thinker in the tradition of the Enlightenment, a period in history that began with the development of modern science during the seventeenth century.

When modern science began to provide an understanding of the world that was separate from superstition and religious belief, there emerged a new faith in the human intellect and its potential for curing the world's ills. The spread of this new-found confidence was aided by the development of the printing press, and by the fact that more and more people could read and write.

In Europe, great Enlightenment philosophers such as John Locke and Jean-Jacques Rousseau argued that monarchical rule was unjust and that political power should reside with the people, not with a king. They believed strongly in the essential goodness of humanity and the power of human reason to gather knowledge, to understand and live in harmony with nature, and ultimately to create a better life for people.

Steeped in this tradition, Thomas Paine had come to America sponsored by Benjamin Franklin. The two men had met in England. In *Common Sense* the radical pamphleteer harshly criticized England's King George III, whom he called a "wretch . . . with the pretended title of father of his people." He also condemned the very idea of hereditary rule and staunchly advocated liberal democracy.

A thirst for absolute power is the natural disease of monarchy . . . In England a King hath little more to do than to make war and give away places; which in plain terms, is to impoverish the nation . . . A pretty business indeed for a man to be allowed eight hundred thousand pounds sterling a year for, and worshipped into the bargain! Of more worth is one honest man to society and in the sight of God, than all the crowned ruffians that ever lived.

Paine argued in favor of the right of all people to free themselves from the tyranny of foreign domination through whatever means necessary, and he was the first to call openly for Americans to liberate themselves from the British Crown. A radical in the truest and best sense of the word, Paine declared,

> We have it in our power to begin the world over again . . . 'Tis not the concern of a day, a year, or an age; posterity are virtually involved in the contest, and will be more or less affected even to the end of time, by the proceedings now. Now is the seed-time of the Continental union.

Many colonists read Paine's words with enthusiasm. Jefferson found himself in agreement with many of Paine's liberal ideas which were considered very radical at the time. It is surprising that Jefferson, the son of a successful businessman, was attracted to the radical thought of Thomas Paine. Some have attributed this to the ultimate truth of Paine's ideas and Jefferson's reverence for the truth. Together, Paine and Jefferson provided the inspiration and some of the determination necessary to make revolution a reality in America.

3

The Struggle for Independence

"RESOLVED: THAT THESE United Colonies are, and of right ought to be, free and independent States, that they are absolved from all allegiance to the British Crown, and that all political connection between them and the State of Great Britain is, and ought to be, totally dissolved. . . ."

Richard Henry Lee, the Virginia delegate to the Second Continental Congress, wrote these stirring words in June 1776. Lee's sentiments were shared by a growing number of delegates, but some still believed that the best course to take would be a compromise with England. That month the Congress appointed a committee to draft a statement arguing the case for American independence. Jefferson, the best writer of the five delegates chosen to serve on the committee, was invited to compose the first draft.

The draft not only had to convey the sense of urgency felt by Americans throughout the colonies, but it also had to serve as an inspiration for the long struggle that lay ahead. Jefferson gathered everything within the power of his heart and mind to present in a clear, concise way the argument for American independence. The result—The Declaration of Independence—denounced the British Crown, proclaimed the end of tyranny in America, and offered hope for the founding of a free nation.

When the Declaration came before the Congress, Jefferson listened anxiously as the delegates hotly debated its contents word by word. The process of carefully editing and revising was painstaking and time consuming, as each delegate sought to modify the document. Jefferson felt each revision like a battle wound. In the end he thought that the document was weakened by the delegates' changes.

On July 4, 1776, the written Declaration was approved by the Continental Congress. Then, on August 2, in a ceremony that to this day marks perhaps the single most important moment in American history, John Hancock of Massachusetts, president of the Congress, stepped forward to sign the parchment on which the Declaration of Independence was written. One by one, all 56 delegates signed. In the eyes of their fellow colonists, they were brave men who had taken a stand for liberty. These men had put their lives on the line for their new country. In the eyes of the British Crown they were traitors—and subject to death by hanging.

His work on the Declaration completed, Jefferson was anxious to get back to Monticello. His wife's health had worried him all the time he was in Philadelphia. He returned home a hero. Although the fact that Jefferson had written the Declaration did not become public knowledge until later, people in high political circles in the colonies acknowledged his authorship. Once back in Albemarle County, Jefferson was delighted to be home with his family. He happily resumed his various projects on his grand plantation.

Jefferson spent most of 1777 with his family in Monticello, planting and building with astounding vigor. His diary reveals that he planted acres of trees. However Jefferson was not entirely consumed by physical labor. The experience of writing the Declaration of Independence forced him to examine his own life in relation to the high principles he had expressed in the document. When he did so, he became troubled.

The idea that all men are created equal was central to the Declaration of Independence. Every man is born with the right to life, liberty, and the pursuit of happiness. How then, thought Jefferson, can slavery be justified? Slaves from Africa made up an important part of the labor force on Jefferson's plantation, and throughout the South. They comprised almost half of Virginia's population of 400,000, and nearly 200 slaves worked at Monticello.

Jefferson knew that if he'd condemned slavery in the Declaration he would be open to charges of hypocrisy. Still, how could a man who had so passionately espoused the ideas of freedom and democracy also be a slavemaster? In his writings he criticized slaveholders for their often harsh treatment of their slaves, but he allowed his own runaway slaves to be severely punished when they were caught. Jefferson supported a law aimed at abolishing slavery in Virginia, but he kept most of his own slaves after such a law was passed. He simply did not practice what he preached on the issue of slavery.

31

Jefferson's slaves made Monticello possible. They not only built and maintained the house and tended the crops, but they cooked for the family and cared for the Jefferson children. Jefferson had inherited hundreds of slaves—yet the idea of human property was alien to the principles of liberty and justice that Jefferson held dear. He had put antislavery passages in the original draft of the Declaration, but these were removed by Southern delegates, who, like Jefferson, were from slave states and were slaveholders themselves. The matter of slavery would weigh heavily on Jefferson's conscience all his life.

Jefferson was aware that the issue had to be resolved sooner or later. He was also concerned about other issues of great importance at the time. One of them was land reform.

The bulk of the land in the colony of Virginia had been owned by a handful of families for many generations. Jefferson believed that such exclusive land ownership was inappropriate in a democracy. In the Virginia Assembly he had supported legislation aimed at redistributing the land among a greater number of people.

Jefferson thought that owning land through inheritance was much the same as Thomas Paine's view on hereditary rule—it was undemocratic tyranny over the masses. As with slavery, Jefferson's own substantial inheritance was at odds with his liberal ideas about land reform. Clearly he struggled with the slavery and land reform issues on two levels—the practical and the intellectual. He was never able to reconcile the two.

Another important issue to Jefferson was a person's right to worship as he or she pleases. Jefferson

The Bettmann Archive

Monticello, Jefferson's beloved home in Virginia. The name means "little hill" in Italian. After Shadwell, the original plantation house, burned down in 1770, Jefferson choose the site and designed the new house himself. He kept adding to it and changing it for over forty years. Today, it is open to visitors as one of America's most cherished museums.

believed in the separation of church and state, that no one religion should be favored by the government, and that no citizen should be forced to support or practice a religion not of his or her own choosing. Like Thomas Paine, Jefferson was not a religious man in any conventional sense. He thought that religion was a personal matter, and should not be subject to government regulation.

Though the colonists originally came to America to escape religious persecution in England, Jefferson's liberal ideas on religious freedom met a great deal of resistance. The church of England, or Anglican church, was very powerful in Virginia and did not want to share its influence with other religious groups. Despite this, Jefferson was determined to make freedom of religion a reality in the colonies, not just empty words preserved in the Declaration of Independence. For years he fought for legislation that would recognize the individual's right to choose his or her own form of worship and to practice it without fear of persecution. Eventually, in 1786, after a long and bitter debate, such a law would be passed in Virginia.

Another issue that was very important to Jefferson was public education. He recognized the importance of having educated citizens in a democracy. It does little good for a nation to be free if it remains ignorant. Thomas Jefferson supported the idea of a public educational system, one that everyone could go to regardless of how much money or status they had. Access to the works of the world's great philosophers, scientists, and literary artists, Jefferson believed, was essential for people to govern themselves in an informed and enlightened way. He urged that a Virginia state library be built and that it offer free borrowing privileges to all citizens.

While Jefferson was fighting on the legislative front in the Virginia Assembly, young colonial soldiers fighting for the same ideals as Jefferson were dying on America's battlefields. Great Britain's strategy was to isolate New England from the rest of the colonies. Rebellious sentiment was strongest there. The British generals planned on taking New York and New Jersey in one quick blow. To do so, they landed more than 250 ships and 30,000 troops on Staten Island in the summer of 1776.

Under the leadership of British General William Howe, the English troops were well trained and well equipped. General George Washington, commander-in-chief of the American forces, had only 10,000 troops at his disposal. Food was scarce, their clothing was tattered, and often they were without boots. Washington's rag-tag group was a sorry sight and certainly no match for Howe's finely tuned ranks.

In August, when British and colonial troops clashed at Brooklyn Heights, General Washington and his troops were forced to retreat across the East River into Manhattan. Then in November the British captured Fort Washington in northern Manhattan and Fort Lee across the Hudson River in New Jersey. Nearly 3,000 troops and officers were forced to surrender. Washington led his battered troops on a hasty and confused retreat across New Jersey that winter.

The cold weather became an important factor in the war. The American troops, dressed mostly in shredded uniforms with their feet wrapped in rags, suffered severe cases of frostbite when they were forced to camp along the western bank of the Delaware River. The British had warm lodging in Trenton, New Jersey. Morale among the American ranks reached a terrible low, while the British plotted their advance on Philadelphia from Trenton.

Then in a bold and desperate move, Washington planned a surprise attack. On December 25, 1776, Washington's army boarded wooden boats and began a perilous journey across the icy Delaware River. Carrying more than 150 pieces of artillery through bitter cold and driven snow, the Americans marched quietly for nine miles through the darkness toward Trenton and the British camp.

In the early morning hours of December 26, they attacked the sleeping British troops and then escaped just before enemy reinforcements arrived. On January 3, 1777 American troops were victorious in another confrontation in Princeton, New Jersey. Then they took refuge near Morristown. Washington's bold stroke had saved the American movement for independence.

The necessity for more manpower gave rise to numerous campaigns throughout the northern colonies to enlist slaves for military service. In exchange for their service, slaves were offered freedom, as in Massachusetts, and sometimes land grants, as in New York. Their masters were compensated monetarily for each slave taken by the government. Soon several states had trained "black battalions" ready to go into battle.

Though initially against the idea of recruiting blacks, General Washington gradually came to respect the black recruits for their courage and skill in battle. He urged the southern states to recruit blacks as the northern states had done, particularly as casualties mounted and the ranks of colonial militiamen dwindled. Eventually, Congress recommended that 3,000 black troops be raised in South Carolina and Georgia, providing funds to compensate the slavemasters $1,000 for each slave recruited.

Resistance to the idea of slave recruitment in the South was strong. The idea of 3,000 black slaves trained in military methods and issued firearms scared a good many southerners, including Jefferson. Obviously they feared that such a state of affairs could only lead to a slave rebellion. James Madison was one southerner who favored the idea of black recruitment, but he was in a definite minority in the South. Despite this resistance, tens of thousands of blacks fought for American independence, and many lost their lives in battle. The recruitment of blacks for military service proved to be an important step toward their ultimate emancipation during President Abraham Lincoln's term.

Even with substantial black enlistment, the colonial forces remained a sorry lot compared to the British forces. Still, the Americans had two important advantages. America's rough, open terrain made the traditional British style of warfare impractical. And in the American colonists, England's soldiers faced an opponent whose will to win was greater than their own.

Safe and secure at Monticello, Jefferson followed reports from the battle fronts and was dismayed to read of the terrible hardships of the war, the heavy casualties, and the battered hopes of the brave men who were fighting for America's freedom. Many criticized Jefferson for his willingness to stay out of harm's way during this time of national crisis. While Americans were dying fighting for many of the ideas he shared, in a war that he helped to declare, Jefferson remained on his lovely country estate with his orange trees, his vegetable garden, his telescopes, and his books.

Jefferson was not uncaring, and if called upon would have been willing to make great personal sacrifices for the cause of American independence. But he did not have the power to stop the suffering and hardship. Nor would he have been able to bring about an end to the fighting. Moreover, he was not a military man. He was a man of ideas and of the pen. The most valuable contribution he could make to the American cause was more likely to be on the page than on the battlefield.

On the battle front, British General John Burgoyne's forces advanced on Albany in upstate New York, while General Howe's troops approached Philadelphia. On Sept. 11, 1777, Howe's 15,000 troops clashed with the 11,000 American troops on the northern banks of the Brandywine Creek. The Americans suffered more than 1,000 casualties before being forced to retreat. Howe took Philadelphia without firing a shot.

The fighting in upstate New York continued. John Burgoyne and his army of 8,000 had marched up the west bank of the Hudson River only to be ambushed by the American militia. The main American army of 2,000 men under the command of Horatio Gates was barricaded behind strong fortifications, 25 miles north of Albany. Two thousand British troops attacked the colonists at Freeman's Farm but were turned back. Then on October 17, 1777, Burgoyne, surrounded and with no hope of reinforcements, surrendered at Saratoga.

When news of the American victory at Saratoga reached Paris, France, in early December, the French decided to help the Americans fight the British. Despite the recent victories, the Continental Army was still hanging on by a thread. New supplies and funds were desperately needed for the army to continue the war. Now, with the help of the French, the colonists believed they might be able to tilt the balance of power in their favor.

Hoping for better luck than they'd recently had in New England, the British advanced on the South. In December 1778 Savannah, Georgia fell to the British. The following May, a British fleet struck Virginia at Hampton Roads and Portsmouth.

Virginia's defenses were a shambles. The state had very little money in its treasury and only a small, poorly equipped militia. In June 1779 the Virginia legislature appointed Thomas Jefferson governor.

With the British advancing, Governor Jefferson immediately set about gathering soldiers, obtaining supplies, and enlisting the aid of trained commanders. Finally he had been thrust into the front lines of the war. Though the chances of a colonial victory appeared slim, Jefferson was determined to fight the odds.

Martha Jefferson, the governor's wife, had been asked by Martha Washington, the general's wife, to participate in a drive to raise funds and make clothing for the colonial soldiers. Despite her fragile health and a series of difficult pregnancies, Martha Jefferson agreed. In August 1780 she wrote a letter to Eleanor Madison, the wife of James Madison, asking her to help as well. The letter shows the same determination that Thomas Jefferson displayed.

"I undertake with cheerfulness," Martha wrote, "the duty of furnishing to my country women an opportunity of proving that they also participate of those virtuous feelings which gave birth to it."

In January 1781 British troops led by Benedict Arnold stormed Virginia by land and sea. They advanced on Richmond, Virginia, the seat of state government. Governor Jefferson was forced to flee with his family to Tuckahoe, where he remained for several days. The British left Richmond after only a single day, but not before destroying much of the city in a 66-mile rampage. They burned mills, factories, homes, and stores. They also managed to take with them wagon loads of weapons and munitions, which the Virginia militia was already sorely lacking.

When Jefferson crossed the James River and returned to the city, he realized that the loss of all the muskets and gunpowder had made the Virginia militia helpless. Before the year was out, British forces had overrun the pathetic Virginia defenses.

Historians generally agree that Jefferson's two terms as governor were disastrous, though not for lack of diligence. Jefferson himself seems to have preferred to forget that period in his life. In his *Autobiography,* he devotes only a few paragraphs to a discussion of his work as governor.

With the public morale at a desperate low in Virginia, Jefferson wrote to Washington, admitting his failure, expressing his regret, and informing the general that he would not seek a third term as Virginia's governor. He returned to Monticello dejected and swore he would never again run for, or accept an appointment to, public office.

Jefferson would leave the governor's post in bitter defeat in June 1781, but the election to decide his replacement was delayed for two days, slightly extending his term. Thus, he was still governor on June 2, when he was awakened at sunrise by a young man named Jack Jouett.

Perspiring, out of breath, and a bit delirious, Jouett had spent the night traveling to Monticello on horseback in order to bring important news. His face was badly scratched by dense brush he had ridden through in the forests along the way. Jouett told Jefferson that he had been at the Cuckoo Tavern in Raleigh the night before. He had overheard a British plan to capture the Virginia legislature and take Jefferson prisoner.

Jefferson sent Martha and the children to safety and sat down to breakfast, all the while scanning the hills through his telescope. When he saw the raiding force of Banastre Tarleton through his scope, Jefferson quickly mounted his horse and made his escape into the forest toward Carter's Mountain.

Jefferson fled, believing he would return to Monticello only to find a pile of smoldering timbers and ash. Possibly struck by the beauty of the place, the British did not destroy it—at least not immediately. Though the first raiding party holed up at Monticello for 18 hours, they left without doing any damage or harming slaves. However as General Charles Cornwallis's troops swept through Virginia, they burned fences, barns, and crops; abducted slaves; carried off farm animals; and cut the throats of colts too young to ride into battle. Much of Jefferson's property was devastated, but the house at Monticello survived.

Considered a traitor by the British, and alone against an entire army, Jefferson would have been a fool not to retreat when he did. Still, in later years many of his critics recalled the incident as evidence of cowardice. Though outraged by the suggestion that what he had done under the circumstances was cowardly, for years Jefferson never defended himself against such critics. Then in true Jeffersonian fashion, he put the accusation to rest with the following ironic reference to *Don Quixote:*

> That it has been sung in verse, and said in humble prose that, forgetting the noble example of the hero of La Mancha, and his windmills I declined a combat, singly against a troop, in which victory would have been so glorious? Forgetting, themselves, at the same time, that I was not provided with the enchanted arms of the knight, nor even with his helmet of Mabrino. These closet heroes forsooth would have disdained the shelter of a wood, even singly and unarmed, against a legion of armed enemies.

The situation was dire in Virginia at the end of Jefferson's second term as governor. Not only had the state been ravaged by war, but Jefferson himself was now under scrutiny for his poor performance. A formal inquiry began in the Virginia legislature on June 12, 1781, and Jefferson had a hard time coming up with adequate answers to some difficult questions.

He went into seclusion at his Poplar Forest plantation, 90 miles from Monticello. While riding Caractacus, one of his horses, he was thrown. He sustained some serious injuries from which it took him more than a month to recover. Jefferson was an excellent horseman. Having raised Caractacus from a colt, he knew the horse well. It was a freak accident, but one with symbolic meaning, for Caractacus is the name of an ancient British king.

The other colonies fared better against the British than Virginia that year. An American offensive successfully drove the British forces out of Georgia and the Carolinas. British General Cornwallis and his army retreated to Yorktown, Virginia, where they entrenched behind massive fortifications. When the British tried to rescue Cornwallis's troops by sea, they were turned back by a French fleet.

Washington, concluding that the French had eliminated any chance of a British escape by sea, joined with the French troops under the command of the Marquis de Lafayette to trap the British forces at Yorktown and attack from all sides. They were successful. On October 19, 1781, Cornwallis surrendered. Though Congress was not to officially proclaim an end to the war until April 17, 1783, America's independence was essentially won at Yorktown.

The Battle at Yorktown marked the end of British oppression in the colonies, and it paved the way for the establishment, for the first time in history, of a new nation founded on the notion of liberal democracy—freedom, equality, justice, and a government elected by the people. This was the ideal that Jefferson had charted in the Declaration of Independence, the dream that fueled the colonial rebellion from start to finish.

Jeffersonian democracy—as American historians sometimes refer to this ideal—became the cornerstone of the United States of America, the basis of its constitution, and the guiding light for many decades to come. It would also inspire and motivate people of other nations to seek their independence and struggle for their own freedom from oppression. Indeed, Jefferson himself came to symbolize this ideal at home and around the world.

In 1782 Jefferson suffered another personal tragedy. His wife Martha, who had borne a child, Lucy Elizabeth, that May, never regained her strength. Through the summer her condition worsened, and Jefferson remained with her, either at her bedside or writing in an adjacent room. She sensed that she was dying. It has been said that she asked Jefferson to promise he would never remarry after her death, because she didn't want another woman raising their children. Some believe Jefferson made that promise. If he did, he kept it.

Martha died on September 6, 1782, at 11:45 in the morning. Despite the efforts of his daughters to console him, Jefferson was deeply saddened by his wife's death. Moreover, the baby, Lucy Elizabeth, would not survive infancy.

Eventually Jefferson took on a writing project to distract himself from his grief. The result was *Notes on the State of Virginia,* a detailed portrait of Jefferson's native state. Steeped in Virginia's history, laws, and customs, Jefferson was able to create a marvelous work, not only filled with a wide range of factual information but incorporating his personal vision and philosophy as well.

With *Notes,* Jefferson quickly established himself

both in Europe and in the colonies as more than a politician. He was recognized as a philosopher, scientist, and man of letters. Moreover, like Thomas Paine, Jefferson was a true man of the Enlightenment.

4

The Young Diplomat

I N MAY 1784 Jefferson was presented with an extraordinary opportunity. Congress appointed him to a three-man commission to go to Paris to meet with representatives of numerous European countries. John Adams and Benjamin Franklin, already in Europe, were the other two men named to the commission. Their purpose was to negotiate commercial treaties that would create channels for profitable trade across the Atlantic Ocean.

That year Jefferson left his youngest daughter with her aunt in Virginia, boarded a ship, and set sail for Europe with his eleven-year-old daughter Martha and his black servant James Hemings.

Their ship landed in Le Havre, France on July 31. They pressed on to the town of Rouen where they spent two days, and then moved up the Seine Valley to the village of Triel, where they stayed the night of August 5. The next day they traveled through numerous French towns and villages with names such as Saint-Germain-en-Laye, Marly, Nanterre, and

Neuilly. They were awed by the charm of these old towns and the splendor of the French countryside.

When they arrived in Paris on August 6, they checked into the Hotel d'Orleans, near the Palais Royal, an important center of Parisian commercial and cultural activity. Then they moved to less expensive lodging—also called the Hotel d'Orleans—on the Left Bank.

Jefferson was immediately struck by the city's incredible beauty and refinement. He took pages and pages of notes on the Parisian architecture, monuments, and the art work in its many museums. He frequently visited the Louvre, the premier museum of Paris, where he was able to view the work of the greatest painters the world has known. One of Jefferson's favorites was called "The Death of Socrates" by the celebrated French painter Jacques-Louis David.

After two months of living out of his luggage in temporary lodgings, Jefferson signed a nine-month lease on a small house on a cul-de-sac on October 16. He began to explore the city in earnest. Every day he spent hours strolling through the city's lovely parks and gardens, walking along the city's winding cobblestone streets, peering into shop windows, and then taking time to select just the right restaurant for his afternoon meal. Parisian chefs, proud of their reputation as the best in the world, took great care to prepare everything to absolute perfection.

Jefferson often engaged Parisian restaurateurs and vintners in discussions on food and wines, wanting to learn as much as he could about French eating habits and the French way of life in general. After ending his meal with a crust of bread, some cheese, and a glass of wine, Jefferson no doubt wandered along the Seine, the lazy river that winds its way through the center of the city. It is said that Jefferson walked some five miles each day he spent in Paris.

One of Jefferson's favorite places to walk was the Bois de Boulogne, a forest located just west of the city. Napoleon had ordered the forest to be landscaped to provide a royal hunting ground, so the beauty of the Bois de Boulogne was preserved while it offered numerous trails for fairly easy trekking. Jefferson spent so many hours walking there that he became a "master of this curious forest," as he wrote to Madame de Corny in the summer of 1787. The Bois de Boulogne, he wrote, "invites you earnestly to come and survey its beautiful verdure, to retire to its umbrage from the heats of the season. I was through it today, as I am every day."

There was one walk in particular that Jefferson made somewhat frequently, particularly during the autumn months of 1787 and 1788. Across the Bois de Boulogne on a hilltop outside the village of Longchamp was a hermitage called Mont Calvaire—a place for hermits to live in solitude away from the cares of normal life. Jefferson often visited the hermitage and its boardinghouse, which the hermits made available as lodging for paying travelers. He took work along with him and sometimes stayed a week or so.

There he could breathe cool, fresh air and indulge in the lovely panoramic view the hilltop offered. He was able to engage in lively, sometimes gossipy conversation, exchange reading materials, and retreat from the tensions of city life.

Books continued to be Jefferson's passion while he

was in Europe. He frequently browsed among the many book stalls that lined the riverbank, chatted with the vendors, and bought books and engravings from them.

"While residing in Paris, I devoted every afternoon I was disengaged, for a summer or two, in examining all the principal bookstores, turning over every book with my own hands, and putting by everything related to America, and indeed whatever was rare and valuable in every science." He maintained standing orders with all the major book sellers in Europe and did a great deal of buying on the Left Bank, where the Paris book trade is even today most active.

Jefferson also was friendly with printers and binders, some of whom he hired to print and bind his own writing. He bought a piano and began to collect sheet music, which he could buy along the Seine at the book stalls. Soon his tiny house was filled with books, art, and music.

From the moment Jefferson moved in, the house was also filled with a good deal of conversation. Jefferson received many guests in Paris, particularly distinguished Americans who were visiting the city. For example, two prominent statesmen, William Short of Virginia and David Humphreys of Connecticut, paid extended visits to Jefferson's house. John Quincy Adams, the son of John and Abigail Adams, also visited frequently.

Jefferson worked hard to improve the trade relations between France and the United States. He later wrote that he was chiefly concerned with "the receipt of our whale oils, salted fish, and salted meats, on favorable terms; the admission of our rice on equal terms with that of Piedmont, Egypt, and the Levant;

a mitigation of the monopolies of our tobacco by the Farmers-general, and a free admission of our production into their islands."

He also devised means by which his newly independent country could pay back the large sum of money France had loaned it during the American War of Independence. For his sterling achievements as a negotiator, Jefferson was appointed ambassador to France by Congress in May 1785. He took over from Benjamin Franklin, who retired at the age of 79 and returned to America in July. John Adams moved on to become America's first ambassador to Great Britain.

Jefferson lived in the house in the cul-de-sac for one year. Then, realizing that his stay in Paris would be an extended one, he moved to a more spacious and considerably more expensive house on the Champs Élysées, at the corner of the rue de Berri. The house was called Hotel de Langeac. It had a lovely garden but was unfurnished, so Jefferson quickly set about furnishing it. He hired additional servants. After acquiring horses and a carriage, he also hired a coachman and several stable hands. Jefferson tended the garden himself, growing grapes, Indian corn, cantaloupe, watermelon, and sweet potato among other crops.

As the American ambassador to France, Jefferson mingled with French aristocrats and other members of the diplomatic corps. He also sought out and befriended celebrated French artists, musicians, writers, scientists, and philosophers. One French artist, the sculptor Jean-Antoine Houdon, greatly impressed Jefferson with his enormous talents, and the two soon became close friends.

When commissioned by the State of Virginia to have a statue of George Washington made, Jefferson approached Houdon. The sculptor had already created a highly acclaimed bust of Benjamin Franklin and was working on one of the French general Lafayette. Jefferson asked Houdon if he would be interested in sculpting George Washington. On July 8, 1785, Houdon agreed to do it. Soon he left for America to sketch the country's famous revolutionary leader, and to make plaster impressions of the general's face.

When Houdon returned to Paris and began to work on the statue, Jefferson frequented the sculptor's studio. He was deeply moved by the beauty of many of the pieces on display there. He especially loved Houdon's bust of the French dramatist Voltaire and his bronze statue of the Greek goddess Diana. Eventually Houdon also created a bust of Jefferson, one that has been admired by many subsequent generations.

While in Paris Jefferson made numerous acquaintances quite unlike those he had made back in America. For instance for the first time in his life Jefferson met and dealt with politically powerful women. This was a very new experience for Jefferson, but for the most part it was not a problem for him. However one politically powerful woman bothered him a great deal—Marie Antoinette, Queen of France. Though he got on splendidly with many celebrities of French society, he developed an early dislike for the French monarchy. When he witnessed the terrible conditions of the French people, who lived in great poverty, that dislike developed into outright hatred.

While in Paris Jefferson kept a watchful eye on events in America. He was particularly interested in the events brought about by a reform movement led by his old friend James Madison. Madison and his supporters believed that the time had come for the loose confederation of former British colonies to become a real nation.

Under the American political structure that was put together when the colonies declared independence, in a document called the Articles of Confederation, each state was to a large degree independent. The central government had no power of taxation and no control over interstate or international commerce. It was unable to pay its loans, which made it very difficult to conduct business with other countries. While the former British colonies were now free, they had not really formed a united country.

Despite their newfound freedom Americans were poorer than they had been under the British. Economic hardship began to threaten the security of the confederation. James Madison and many others believed that real nationhood—and the benefits such status brought with it—would cure America's economic ills. In an effort to acquire that status, the Articles of Confederation had to be revised to provide a stronger central government.

As times became harder, violence erupted in western Massachusetts when a man named Daniel Shays organized a small group of farmers to draw attention to their desperate economic situation. Many American farmers had been put in jail because they were too poor to pay back their loans. In some cases their farms were confiscated by the government because of their debts. When Shays and his mob of angry farmers attempted to capture a federal arsenal, the national government, without a viable army of its own, was helpless to defend its property.

The Massachusetts state militia stepped in and easily put down the uprising, but Shays's rebellion, as the affair came to be called had served two important purposes. It drew attention to the difficult problems facing America's poor farmers, and it showed how powerless the central government was.

When news of Shays's rebellion reached Jefferson in France, his reaction was unusual for an American patriot. Whereas many Americans viewed Shays and his rowdy mates as annoying troublemakers, Jefferson admired the farmers for their courage to stand up to authority. After all, was not this the same kind of spirited action that had severed the colonies' ties with the British?

"I hold it that a little rebellion now and then is a good thing," Jefferson wrote. "It is a medicine necessary for the sound health of government . . . God forbid that we should ever be twenty years without such a rebellion. . . . The tree of liberty must be refreshed from time to time with the blood of patriots and tyrants. It is its natural manure."

Jefferson was torn over the issue of whether or not the Articles of Confederation should be changed to create a stronger central government. He recognized the need to make America more secure and to free it from its financial burdens, but he feared that a powerful central government would become oppressive. For Jefferson, a powerful president at the head of the government was too much like the monarchs of Europe whom he detested. He did not want the reform movement's attempt to achieve stability and security to result in a return to the days of government by a single sovereign.

As the movement for reform of the Articles gained momentum, Congress officially invited representatives from all the states to attend a constitutional convention in Philadelphia. The proceedings began on May 25, 1787, at the Pennsylvania Statehouse. Of the 74 delegates chosen, 19 never attended, and 14 left early. All the states with the exception of Rhode Island sent delegations. The average age of the sitting delegates was 43. Benjamin Franklin, the oldest, was now 81. Jefferson later referred to this body of esteemed men as "an assembly of demigods." George Washington was unanimously elected presiding officer by the members of the convention. Madison and his leading supporter, New York lawyer Alexander Hamilton, were particularly eager to make their case for a strong central government.

The delegates met almost daily for four months of intense debate in the sweltering summer heat. To facilitate free and honest discussion, they took an oath not to discuss what went on within the chamber outside its walls. In fact the windows of the building were kept closed despite the soaring summer temperatures, to discourage would-be eavesdroppers. Because the proceedings were secret, there was no press coverage or public reaction during those months. Because James Madison took detailed notes from his front row seat, which survive to this day, history has a record of the issues discussed and the opinions of various delegates.

The end result of heated and relentless debate at the Convention was a document known as the Con-

stitution of the United States of America. It begins
with the following preamble:

> We the People of the United States, in Order to
> form a more perfect Union, establish Justice, in-
> sure domestic Tranquility, provide for the com-
> mon defence, promote the general Welfare, and
> secure the Blessings of Liberty to ourselves and
> our Posterity, do ordain and establish this Con-
> stitution for the United States of America.

Still in Paris, Jefferson remained somewhat skepti-
cal. He saw the Constitution and the move toward
a stronger central government as an overreaction to
Shays's rebellion. Because the new Constitution provided for a very powerful chief executive officer—the
president—Jefferson was hesitant to endorse it. He
agreed that the central government needed to be able
to raise money through taxes and provide for a strong
national army to defend the country against its enemies. But Jefferson cautioned against making the central government too strong.

Despite his reservations, Jefferson made it clear to
Madison and other American leaders that he thought
the new Constitution should be adopted. He recognized the many benefits of nationhood and the desperate need to unite the former colonies.

Jefferson also made some specific recommendations for the new Constitution. He urged that the president's term be limited to a specified number of years.
Jefferson believed this would guard against one person becoming too powerful and would prevent the
presidency from becoming monarchical rule.

From Paris, Jefferson also urged that Congress add

a bill of rights to the Constitution in which individual rights would be enumerated and guaranteed. In a letter to President Washington, Jefferson cautioned against the tendency of central governments to limit the civil rights of the individual. Others, too, argued for a bill of rights.

Religious groups, for instance, were anxious for the Constitution to include a specific provision forbidding Congress from interfering with the individual's right to free expression of religion. Likewise, publishers urged a Constitutional provision specifically guaranteeing a press that was free from all government interference. In fact the lack of a bill of rights became such a heated issue that it threatened to stall the ratification of the Constitution.

As Jefferson strolled along the banks of the Seine, reflecting on the political developments far away in America, he began to realize that Paris was not simply a beautiful city, full of the excitement of business, government, and culture. Hundreds of thousands of people lived in dreadful squalor, many without even the barest necessities of life. On his many walks he witnessed poverty unlike anything he had ever seen, "more wretched, more accursed in every circumstance of human existence than the most conspicuously wretched individuals of the whole United States."

For more than two centuries the French kings had possessed absolute authority over France, while the nobility and officials of the Roman Catholic Church enjoyed many privileges. Aristocrats received appointments to high government posts, and members of the clergy had broad influence in matters of state. What made matters worse, neither the aristocracy nor the clergy paid taxes. Consequently a heavy tax burden fell on the peasants, who made up the vast majority of the population.

France's involvement in the American War of Independence had so strained France's finances that King Louis XVI urged the aristocracy and clergy to consider tax reform. They rejected the idea, blaming France's financial problems on the monarch's greed and mismanagement. Afraid of opposition from the aristocracy and possible insurrection among the peasantry, Louis borrowed money to pay France's bills. By doing so he quickly doubled the national debt, which made matters even worse.

The people of France began to perceive the king as corrupt, spineless, greedy, incompetent, and entirely incapable of putting France's affairs in order. The overtaxed people were on the verge of rebellion.

Jefferson watched anxiously as tension rose in France, but because of his sensitive diplomatic position, he did not voice his opinion on the critical issues of the day. However he strongly believed in republican government and individual liberties, and he did not consider the hereditary rule of kings a just form of government. He felt that the monarchy ought to be dissolved and that a representative government should replace it. But Jefferson knew from personal experience what enormous commitment and sacrifice was needed to bring about a revolution, and he did not think the downtrodden French masses were ready to make such a commitment and sacrifice.

To his great delight, Jefferson was wrong. On July 14, 1789, a huge crowd stormed the Bastille, the Paris prison that had become a hated symbol of oppression in France. That action began a torrent of revolutionary activity that eventually brought down the king. By the time Jefferson returned to America two months later, the French had established a new national assembly and had adopted many of the principles of the American Revolution, such as human liberty and equality. In fact Jefferson later wrote that the French Revolution was driven by the same revolutionary spirit that had made the American Revolution a reality.

Jefferson returned to America in September 1789 with every intention of returning to Paris after spending some months in Monticello. As it turned out, he would never see Paris again. On April 30 of that year, George Washington had taken the oath of office as the first president of the United States. President Washington knew that the task of forging a nation under the new Constitution would be an extremely difficult one. He immediately set about searching for the most able advisers to join his cabinet. His choice for the nation's first secretary of state was Thomas Jefferson.

5

Secretary of State

AFTER READING PRESIDENT Washington's letter inviting him to become U.S. secretary of state, Jefferson was undecided. Of course every leading patriot of the day would have accepted such an invitation without hesitation. Jefferson certainly realized the offer was not to be taken lightly. But he had intended to be in the United States only briefly, to visit Monticello, put certain affairs in order, and return to Paris. Jefferson was enjoying his work in France, and Paris had become a second home for him. The prospect of leaving his life in Paris behind to move to New York, where the State Department offices were located, was not appealing to him.

James Madison and President Washington both urged Jefferson to accept the post, convinced as they were that he was the best person for the job. He had a wealth of experience, and his experience in foreign relations was great. Still, Jefferson was hesitant, and he expressed his reservation in a letter to the President. He was especially concerned that the administrative duties of the post would be too much of a burden.

Washington responded, expressing his belief that Jefferson was overestimating the administrative work that was required. He also pointed out that Jefferson had the strong support not only of the chief executive but of the American public. Although Jefferson knew that he would pine for the days when he walked along the Seine, he finally accepted the post out of a sense of duty to his country and his president.

After it was announced that Jefferson had become secretary of state and would not be returning to Paris, no fewer than 86 crates containing Jefferson's possessions were packed and shipped to America. Jefferson's horses were sold, and his servants were discharged. It took several months during the summer of 1790 to finish the task of sending Jefferson's clothes, books, wine, art work, scientific instruments, furniture, other household items, and countless souvenirs to America. He had acquired almost all of it during his years in Paris.

U.S. Secretary of State Jefferson left for New York on horseback on March 1, 1790. On the way he spent a week in Richmond, delayed by a snowstorm. Then he stopped in Philadelphia to visit Benjamin Franklin. Aging and bedridden, the celebrated man was living out his last days. That year, Washington, too, became ill and almost died of pneumonia. Jefferson arrived in New York on March 21 and took up residence in a house at 57 Maiden Lane.

For Jefferson, Paris became a fond memory. But his love for France would never fade. Later, Jefferson wrote about that country and its people:

A more benevolent people, I have never known, nor greater warmth and devotedness in their select friendships. Their kindness and accommodations to strangers is unparalleled, and the hospitality of Paris is beyond anything I had conceived to be practicable in a large city. Their eminence, too, in science, the communicative dispositions of their scientific men, the politeness of the general manners, the ease and vivacity of their conversation, give a charm to their society to be found nowhere else.

Indeed, the historian Henry Adams remarked that "with all [Jefferson's] extraordinary versatility of character and opinions, he seemed during his entire life to breathe with perfect satisfaction nowhere except in the liberal, literary, and scientific air of Paris in 1789."

Still, Jefferson was quite pleased to meet his fellow cabinet members in New York—Attorney General Edmund Randolph, Secretary of War Henry Knox, and Secretary of the Treasury Alexander Hamilton. He was greatly impressed by their experience in affairs of state. Hamilton, however, though no less talented than the others, would become Jefferson's bitter political enemy before the year's end.

By brilliance and ingenuity, Alexander Hamilton had risen from impoverished illegitimacy on the Caribbean island of Nevis, where he was born, to prominence as a lawyer, statesman, and man of finance. During the revolution he served in the Continental Army as commander of an artillery unit and then became George Washington's personal secretary and most trusted aide. On December 14, 1780, he married

Elizabeth Schuyler, a daughter of one of New York's wealthiest and most powerful landowners. As America's first secretary of the treasury, Hamilton set out to pay the national debt and restore the country's credit rating with other nations.

By their very natures, Hamilton and Jefferson were antagonistic. Both men had supported America's break with England, both were bright and articulate, and both were patriots and devoted statesmen who had served the country courageously in official capacities. But Hamilton was a military man, a man who lived by the sword. Jefferson was, above all, a man of ideas whose sword was his pen. While Hamilton had been in battle during the Revolution, Jefferson had remained on his Virginia plantation, writing, reflecting, and tending to his vegetables and horses. Moreover Hamilton was a staunch supporter of a strong central government, having little faith in the judgment of the masses. In fact at the Constitutional Convention he argued in favor of almost unlimited federal power. Jefferson, on the other hand, was a man of the people, concerned that a strong central government was likely to endanger individual liberties.

As treasury secretary Hamilton was faced with the difficult task of managing the country's financial affairs. In particular, he was expected to find some means of repaying the enormous debt the government had incurred to finance the War of Independence. To do so, Hamilton devised a plan to raise the money by imposing a federal excise tax on goods manufactured and sold within the United States and an import tax on goods brought into the country from abroad.

Although the secretary of state is supposed to concern himself with foreign policy, Jefferson did not hesitate to voice his opposition to Hamilton's plan. He considered the new taxes an unfair burden on the American people, particularly tradesmen and farmers, who were of very moderate means. Jefferson also feared that under Hamilton's system, the Bank of the United States would acquire too much power over the government. Jefferson further believed that Hamilton's plan so favored the rich that it was essentially corrupt. When he wrote to his brother-in-law "the credit and fate of the nation seem to hang on the desperate throws and plunges of gambling scoundrels," Jefferson was referring, among others, to Hamilton, whom he suspected of misusing government funds.

Their disagreement over federal excise and import taxes was the first but certainly not the only point of contention between Jefferson and Hamilton. In fact the two differed sharply on many issues. But the split between these men was essentially a disagreement on one central question: How much power should be granted to the federal government?

Jefferson argued that the powers of the federal government should be limited to those specifically granted to it by the Constitution, and that all other powers should be reserved for the states. Hamilton, however, interpreted the Constitution more broadly. He believed that the intention of the founding fathers at the Constitutional Convention was to provide a strong national government with constitutional powers that were almost unlimited.

Two schools of thought developed around these very different interpretations of the Constitution. One school, led by Hamilton, John Adams, and George

Washington, became known as the Federalist school. The other, led by Jefferson and James Madison, became known as the Republican school. These two schools eventually gave rise to the first political parties in the United States.

Americans quickly lined up on either side of this deep political chasm, and the result was an intensely divided nation. Each side attacked the other in the press and in public speeches. Members of Congress who had become friends and colleagues suddenly found themselves arguing with each other. Fist fights occurred in taverns and town squares. Friends and family members argued over who was right about the Constitution—Jefferson or Hamilton.

Under various pseudonyms, Hamilton wrote many articles criticizing Jefferson as "the promoter of national disunion, national insignificance, public disorder and discredit." To force Jefferson to resign his post as secretary of state, Hamilton submitted a list of grievances against him to President Washington. Jefferson did not respond personally to Hamilton's attacks but instead enlisted the talents of James Monroe and James Madison.

These two statesmen then collaborated on six essays under the title "Vindication of Mr. Jefferson," published in the *American Daily Advertizer* in late 1793. Jefferson himself wrote a letter to the President accusing Hamilton of meddling in the affairs of the State Department, of launching a campaign against him in the press, and of preferring a hereditary over a republican form of government. He added that working in such a bad atmosphere, he was considering retirement. No doubt he yearned to return to his family and Monticello.

President Washington's patience quickly grew thin. He urged the two men to reconcile their differences. In a letter to Jefferson, Washington wrote, "I believe the views of both of you to be pure and well meant . . . I have a great, sincere esteem and regard for you both, and ardently wish that some line may be marked out by which both of you could walk."

On the issue of Jefferson's retirement, Washington wrote that he, too, eagerly looked forward to retirement but that his duty to his country was above such a consideration. Washington knew full well that there was no individual who could fill Jefferson's shoes. He was hoping to gently shame Jefferson into remaining in his post.

Perhaps George Washington's ploy worked. Jefferson continued to serve as secretary of state. Some historians believe that Jefferson was so afraid that Hamilton would turn the nation into a monarchy that he decided to stay and fight the battle. Whatever the reason for Jefferson's decision, he would not return to the comforts of home and family for some time.

During these volatile political times, the United States government moved to Philadelphia. New York had not yet established itself as a major city, whereas Philadelphia had. Jefferson looked forward to the move, to taking advantage of the city's many cultural offerings. Perhaps, he thought, Philadelphia would relieve him of the yearning he had for his beloved Paris. Indeed, Jefferson found Philadelphia to be a much more agreeable city than New York and was pleased with the move. Philadelphia's museums and libraries, lovely botanical garden, and theater quickly endeared the city to Jefferson.

In the meantime James Madison had been leading a campaign in the House of Representatives to enact a bill of rights to protect people's civil rights. As a result of his efforts, Congress passed 12 amendments to the Constitution in September 1789. Eleven states had to ratify the amendments, however, before they could become law. On December 15, 1791, after much heated debate and compromise among the representatives, 10 amendments were approved, and the Federal Bill of Rights went into effect. Secretary of State Thomas Jefferson had the pleasure of proclaiming its enactment.

In January 1792 Jefferson became a grandfather for a second time when his daughter Martha gave birth to a baby girl, Anne. When he received the news, Jefferson was overcome with both joy and a yearning to be back in Monticello with his family, and he wrote Martha to tell her so. She promptly wrote back, "The anxiety you express to be at home makes me infinitely happy . . . I feel more and more every day how necessary your company is to my happiness by the continual and ardent desire I have of seeing you."

But Jefferson had at least one more year to serve as President Washington's secretary of state. He and his daughter visited infrequently and it was impossible to return to Monticello for any length of time. Jefferson wrote to Martha, "The ensuing year will be the longest of my life, and the last of such hateful labours. The next we will sow our cabbages together."

But 1792 was an election year. President Washington was faced with the decision of whether or not to run for reelection. Like Jefferson, Washington was eager to leave the arena of American politics, to return to his beloved Mount Vernon. Having failed to bring about harmony between Jefferson and Hamilton, the President was tired and frustrated. He told Madison that he would rather "go to his farm, take his spade in his hand, and work for his bread" than serve a second term. Several prominent statesmen, including both Hamilton and Jefferson, urged Washington to serve a second term.

"The confidence of the whole nation is centered on you," Jefferson told the President. Finally Washington agreed to do it. When the ballots were counted, he was reelected. He began his second term, taking the oath of office on March 4, 1793.

By the time Washington and his Vice-President, John Adams, were sworn in, Britain and France were at war. Jefferson naturally supported France, though his opinion was not shared by everyone. As is most often the case, the two new American political parties took opposite sides. Jefferson, Madison, and other Republicans still viewed Britain as a colonial oppressor. They wanted the United States to sever its commercial ties to the British Crown. Many Americans sided with France because the French had helped the American colonists in their struggle for independence from the British. Hamilton and the Federalists, however, believed that it was in the best interest of the United States to work toward improving relations with Britain, which remained a wealthy and influential world power.

The French ambassador, Edmond Genet, came to the United States to seek support for the French effort against the British. He discovered that the American government had taken a position of neutrality. Angered by what he saw as ingratitude, Genet denounced President Washington as a fraud and a traitor to the cause of freedom. In addition, he harshly criticized members of Congress who supported U.S. neutrality. He insisted that the United States owed a degree of allegiance to France and that America was turning its back on a loyal ally in a time of need.

Americans took to the streets to defend the honor of their President against these attacks. Jefferson called the French ambassador's remarks "disrespectful" and "indecent." He publicly called for Genet's immediate dismissal and urged the French government to appoint a new ambassador. Soon Genet's authority was revoked, and he was asked to return home. However political upheaval in France had resulted in the Reign of Terror, in which thousands were being sent to the guillotine for "counterrevolutionary" activities. Fearing that he would lose his head if he returned to France, Genet spent his remaining years on a farm in New York.

As for Jefferson, who was now 50 years old, the Genet affair had soured his love for affairs of state. He contemplated resigning his cabinet post and retiring from public life. On February 27, 1793, he wrote to Madison, "The motion of my blood no longer keeps time with the tumult of the world. It leads me to seek for happiness in the lap and love of my family, in the society of my neighbors and my books, in the wholesome occupations of my farm and my affairs, in an interest or affection in every bud that opens, in every breath that blows around me."

Though it took most of that year for Jefferson to clear his desk of the business he had started as secretary of state, he resigned his post and returned to Monticello that December, looking forward to a peaceful retirement.

6

Down from the Hilltop

JEFFERSON RETIRED TO his secluded hilltop estate. Though he continued to write and receive letters, he had little contact with the outside world, only occasionally visiting with a neighbor or friend. His daughter Martha's husband had developed a mental illness. After the first seven months of Jefferson's retirement, the young couple spent a great deal of time away from Monticello, seeing doctors and visiting health spas. This left Jefferson alone—with several hundred slaves—to tend to the affairs of the vast plantation.

Jefferson was delighted to be at Monticello, where he could amuse himself with his garden, his horses, and his books. He continued to build additions to his lovely house. And he was especially happy to be free of the stressful life he had known when he was active in politics and government. Jefferson remained secluded and blissfully ignorant of political developments during this time, rarely even bothering to pick up a newspaper. He preferred to pass each day surveying his land, overseeing the plantation, or tinkering with his inventions.

Experimenting with new farming techniques, he developed a more efficient plow for tilling the soil, as well as a new method of crop rotation for restoring the fertility of the soil. He planted an extensive garden of herbs and vegetables as well as 1,157 peach trees, recording the details of these accomplishments in his *Garden Book*. Jefferson also established a small nail factory, which produced some 10,000 nails a day.

When not so occupied, Jefferson spent many hours each day on horseback, slowly following the gently sloped trails that wound through his acreage. He continued to shy away from political debate. He wrote to Madison, "I never shall take another newspaper of any sort. I find my mind totally absorbed in my rural occupations."

Jefferson did not remain oblivious to national affairs for very long, however. In fact, he criticized farmers and laborers who did not at least make some effort to be informed of current political events. In view of widespread apathy among American farmers and workers, Jefferson began to have serious doubts about his belief in participatory government. If the common person was so badly informed, how could he be relied on to make sound political choices at the polls?

Not all farmers were apathetic. In July 1794, when a group of Pennsylvania farmers and whiskey makers armed themselves to protest whiskey taxes, Jefferson watched with great interest. They attacked federal tax offices, as well as farmers who agreed to pay the tax. Remembering Shays's Rebellion, Jefferson admired the spirit of these Pennsylvania farmers, who were no longer able to endure the heavy tax burden placed on them by the federal government.

Hamilton and other Federalists, however, condemned the uprising as a threat to the nation's security. They characterized the protestors as trouble-makers who were willing to resort to violence at the slightest whim. President Washington easily put down the revolt with 15,000 militiamen.

Though no lives were lost in the ordeal, Jefferson and the Republicans condemned the government action as "an armament against people and their ploughs." Jefferson attacked the Federalists for what he perceived as their insensitivity to the problems of common people. He also criticized Washington for overreacting. When the nation's poorest citizens rebel, Jefferson wrote in a letter to a friend, it is sometimes because they are heavily burdened and deprived of a decent living. He argued that the Pennsylvania "whiskey boys," as they were called, were not a threat to national security, that their goal was not to overthrow the state but rather to force the government to acknowledge their predicament and to do something about it. Ordering troops to put down the rebellion, Jefferson protested, was a gross violation of the farmers' Constitutional rights.

With his second term coming to an end, President George Washington was able to claim many successes. A treaty with Spain had given the United States the right to navigate the entire length of the Mississippi River and to use the port of New Orleans. Three new states, Kentucky, Tennessee, and Vermont, had joined the union. There were plans for a new national capital on the Potomac River, north of Mount Vernon.

In 1796 Washington decided he would not run for a third term. Though he was sure to be elected, he was now 64 years old. He had served his country well. He was ready to retire.

Washington's farewell address, delivered in New York on September of that year, remains one of the most important documents in American history. In many ways it set the tone and direction for many subsequent administrations. He urged the American people to put aside their differences and to take pride in their country. In foreign affairs, he encouraged America to observe "good faith and justice toward all nations" and to "steer clear of permanent alliances." This speech set the stage for a heated 1796 presidential campaign, a hard-fought battle between the Republicans and the Federalists.

Vice-President John Adams had already made clear his desire to become president as the Federalist candidate. A Harvard-educated lawyer, Adams had served as a member of the Continental Congress and had assisted Jefferson in writing the Declaration of Independence. He was widely admired for his patriotism and high moral principles. More than any other Federalist, Adams seemed the logical choice to succeed Washington as president of the United States.

The Republicans, however, had more of a problem selecting their candidate. The two most qualified men from their party were Madison and Jefferson. Unfortunately, each wanted to see the other become president. Madison insisted that Jefferson make a bid for office, while Jefferson claimed to lack the energy and the desire either to run or to govern. Still, most believed that Jefferson was the best man for the job. His reputation as a brilliant thinker, a shrewd diplomat, and a man of strong moral principle was unequalled. Few doubted that Jefferson would be a great president. Even the Federalists admitted that Jefferson would be a formidable opponent for Adams.

The Republicans would not take "no" for an answer. They began a feisty campaign to elect Jefferson president of the United States. He was touted as a true man of the people who had defended the rights of the common man on numerous occasions. Of course Jefferson was already known as the writer of the Declaration of Independence, and his campaign strategists wasted no opportunity to underscore that fact as well as other Jeffersonian virtues. By contrast, Adams was portrayed as a product of northern wealth and privilege, eager to subordinate the rights of states and their citizens to the power of the federal government.

Madison and Aaron Burr, a lawyer from New York who had built a reputation on his opposition to Alexander Hamilton, led the Republican strategy. Jefferson, meanwhile, remained in Monticello, merely watching the campaign unfold from a distance. The Federalists countered, attacking Jefferson's character and reputation. They claimed that Jefferson was a man of ideas, not a leader, and one who had recently shown disdain for politics and government. They recalled his flawed performance as governor of Virginia, and they suggested his love for France would color his foreign policy decisions.

When the votes were counted, Adams had won 71 electoral votes to Jefferson's 68, split along northern and southern lines. John Adams became the second president of the United States. Today presidential candidates select vice-presidential running mates from their own political party. In 1796, however, the person who received the second highest number of votes in the presidential election became vice-president. As a result the country now had a Federalist president, John Adams, and a Republican vice-president, Thomas Jefferson.

In February 1797, Jefferson once more left the comfortable surroundings of Monticello and journeyed to Philadelphia. Reuniting with Adams was like striking up an old—although sometimes strained—friendship. For years the two had respected and admired each other, and had even fought for many of the same beliefs.

Though the two statesmen were not without their differences, Adams and Jefferson proved to be above the bitter Federalist-Republican rivalry that characterized the political climate of the day. This good will, however, was not to last.

One episode that underscored their differences occurred in May 1797. In an effort to open up better relations between France and the United States, Adams appointed a three-man commission to negotiate a treaty with the French. In France the American ministers were at first ignored. Then they were told by emissaries from the French foreign minister, Charles Talleyrand—the emissaries were identified in the commission's dispatches as X, Y, and Z—that it would cost the United States $250,000 to speak with Talleyrand. The U.S. commission refused to pay a fee to negotiate with the French. The XYZ Affair, as it became known in the press, reinforced the anti-French sentiment among some Federalists. It also produced "such a shock in the Republican mind," according to Jefferson, "as had never been seen since our independence."

The Adams administration took measures to prepare for war with France. First all existing treaties with France were repudiated. Then, in the spring and summer of 1798 Congress authorized the capture of armed French ships, appropriated funds to strengthen the national defenses, and outlawed all commercial trade with France. Numerous confrontations between French and American ships followed, but the two countries never officially declared war. The government also sought to censor pro-French Republicans such as Thomas Jefferson.

In this highly charged political climate, the loyalties of many Europeans visiting or residing in the United States were suddenly suspect. Some were even suspected of spying. This fear of foreigners led the Federalist-dominated Congress to pass the Alien and Sedition Acts in 1799. Two separate pieces of legislation, the Acts provided for the imprisonment of enemy aliens during wartime, required a residence period of 14 years before an immigrant could apply for citizenship, authorized the president to deport foreigners he considered dangerous to the country's security, and established penalties for "any false, scandalous, and malicious writing or writings against the government of the United States, or the President of the United States, with intent to defame . . . or to bring . . . either of them into contempt or disrepute."

Passage of the Alien and Sedition Acts was clearly a partisan attempt by the Federalists to silence Republicans. Jefferson, appalled at the affront to individual liberties the Acts represented, attacked the measures as violations of the basic freedoms guaranteed by the Constitution. A citizen's fundamental right to freedom of speech and a free press, he argued, cannot be denied by the government. The Constitution will not stand for censorship!

As a Republican vice-president in a Federalist administration, it was difficult for Jefferson to criticize government policies. He could be thrown out of government or even accused of treason. He decided to attack the Alien and Sedition Acts with an anonymous statement. It became known as the Kentucky Resolutions because Jefferson had arranged for it to be presented to the state legislature of Kentucky in 1799. Eventually it was printed and distributed throughout the United States.

In the Resolutions Jefferson declared that the Alien and Sedition Acts were unconstitutional and unenforceable. He fell short of advocating open rebellion against the government over the legislation. The Kentucky Resolutions were an impassioned defense of states' rights and individual liberties, and a plea for a more effective check on federal power. Also, the Resolutions amounted to a direct assault on Adams. For this reason, 5,000 copies of the statement were distributed during the presidential campaign of 1800.

The XYZ Affair and the furor over the Alien and Sedition Acts had lessened Adams's influence in Congress. His most loyal Federalist colleagues in the legislature had wanted a declaration of war against France, which Adams had wisely decided to avoid. The Republicans were harboring resentment over the Alien and Sedition Acts. The presidential election campaign of 1800 promised to be a heated one.

That year, the seat of the U.S. government was

moved from Philadelphia to a newly created district, the District of Columbia, on the Potomac River between Virginia and Maryland. Jefferson had favored the new location because it was located halfway between the northern and southern states. The new capital was little more than a flat, muddy, and desolate field, but Jefferson believed that in one important respect the place was ideal. Because it was virtually untouched, every detail of the new city could be planned right from the start. Jefferson got right to work, making architectural and other recommendations for the buildings of the new capital, which eventually would be named Washington, after the nation's first president.

Jefferson, now 57 years old, plunged himself into the task of defeating the Federalists in the presidential elections. Adams and his party, led by campaign manager Alexander Hamilton, were formidable opponents. Hamilton denounced Jefferson as "an atheist, a modern French philosopher, overturner of Government," while Jefferson worked steadfastly behind the scenes to counter the Federalist attacks. He made full use of his great influence with men in government and the press, who published articles defending Jefferson's character and qualifications, supporting his positions, and criticizing his opponent.

Jefferson wrote letters to important people and even distributed political pamphlets himself. A campaign biography was printed and several thousand copies were distributed. At Republican rallies the following song was sung again and again by Jefferson supporters:

Rejoice, Columbia's sons rejoice
To tyrants never bend the knee
But join with heart and soul and voice
For Jefferson and Liberty
From Georgia up to Lake Champlain
From seas to Mississippi's shore
Ye sons of freedom loud proclaim
The reign of terror is no more

Even after the polls opened, both parties continued their efforts to win. Party representatives spoke to voters at the polling places, and the candidates themselves even engaged in public debates. When the polls closed and the votes were counted, Thomas Jefferson had defeated John Adams.

Still, victory was not yet Jefferson's. Aaron Burr, Jefferson's running mate, had received 73 electoral votes, the same number of electoral votes as Jefferson. This tie vote created an uncertainty as to whether Jefferson or Burr was the people's choice for president. Such a tie could not occur today because now delegates to the electoral college cast their votes for a "ticket," which includes both a presidential and a vice-presidential candidate. Though the electoral system in 1800 did not guard against a tie, it did provide for a means of breaking one in the event that it occurred. The House of Representatives had to choose between the two men by voting.

Burr was a man of mixed reputation. He clearly possessed a keen intellect and a persuasive personal charm, but many considered him to be overly ambitious and driven by fantasy. Though Burr had served in the army during the Revolutionary War, his most notable act as a soldier was one of insubordination, which he committed while serving under General Henry Knox. Burr was small in stature, but his manner was grandiose, and he stood ready to be America's next president.

Thirty-five roll calls were taken over a period of five days, including one all-night session. Delegates grew tired and frustrated by the deadlock. Still no decision was made. Jefferson supporters, angered by what they saw as Burr's attempt to steal the election, protested outside the hall of Congress, and Burr supporters hoped that Congress would decide in favor of their candidate. Finally, on the sixth day and the 36th roll call, the majority of delegates voted for Thomas Jefferson. He was now the third president of the United States of America.

7

President Jefferson

THOMAS JEFFERSON WAS inaugurated as the third president of the United States in Washington, D.C., on March 4, 1801. Plainly dressed, he walked to the Capitol, took the oath of office, and delivered his inaugural address in the Senate chamber that morning. Calling for a bipartisan effort to work for the good of the country, Jefferson declared, "We are all Republicans; we are all Federalists."

He then emphasized his belief in the rights of the individual, particularly the right to free speech and the liberal exchange of ideas, by saying, "If there be any among us who would wish to dissolve this Union or to change its republican form, let them stand undisturbed as monuments of the safety with which error of opinion may be tolerated where reason is left free to combat it." In other words, Jefferson was saying that even if people disagreed with the government of the United States, they were entitled to that opinion. He went on to say, "I know, indeed, that some honest men fear that a republican government cannot be strong. . . . I believe this, on the contrary, the strongest government on earth . . . a wise and frugal government, which shall restrain men from injuring one another, which shall leave them otherwise free to regulate their own pursuits of industry and improvement, and shall not take from the mouth of labor the bread it has earned."

Jefferson wisely surrounded himself with extremely able cabinet officers. He asked James Madison to be secretary of state. Henry Dearborn was Jefferson's selection for secretary of war, and his choice for attorney general was Levi Lincoln, both from New England. Albert Gallatin, a Swiss-born financial expert of wide and solid reputation, became secretary of the treasury. After some deliberation, Robert Smith of Baltimore was named secretary of the navy.

Jefferson moved into the recently built president's mansion on Pennsylvania Avenue. It was a spacious and handsome house, but Jefferson was not comfortable there. He did everything he could to make the house a home. He brought in furnishings, installed and modified various fixtures to suit his taste, and spent many hours landscaping. But his new residence remained cold and impersonal no matter what he did. He missed Monticello.

One aspect of the house that bothered Jefferson was its enormous size. Even compared to Monticello, a relatively large house in its day, the White House was palatial, and Jefferson had trouble filling it alone. Because his wife had died, there was no first lady. Jefferson's daughters were living in Virginia raising their own families, and his small staff barely occupied part of a single wing of the great mansion. Jefferson often received guests and had large dinner parties. For a short time James Madison and his wife Dolley stayed at the White House, but for President Jefferson these diversions provided only temporary relief from the feeling that something was missing in his life. The new city of Washington, D.C., only made matters worse. Though Jefferson had initially recognized the many advantages to moving the capital to its present site and had supported the change, he was not happy living there. The city, new, unfinished, and unsettled, consisted of little more than a few partly built government buildings separated by flat, muddy fields and swamps. For a man who had grown accustomed to the great cultural offerings of Paris and Philadelphia, this fledgling capital had precious little to offer. Yearning for more comfortable and familiar surroundings, Jefferson frequently made the 100-mile journey from Washington to Monticello, where he could forget affairs of state and lose himself in his books and his inventions.

Jefferson wanted to direct the United States on a course of fiscal responsibility by cutting federal spending and thus reducing the national debt. He also felt it important that the international tensions that the policies of the Adams administration had created, particularly with France and Britain, be calmed. These long-term objectives would concern him throughout his presidency, but there were also more immediate problems to resolve.

One such problem concerned the Federalist influence in the nation's courts. During his last hours before leaving office, President John Adams had appointed 16 judges, all Federalists, to sit on the federal bench. It was Adams's hope that the appointment of these "midnight judges" (they were called this because they were appointed so late in Adams's term) would block Jefferson from appointing Republicans. They could ensure that Federalist thinking would color the decisions of the courts for years and possibly decades to come.

By the time Jefferson took office, the commissions for the judges had been signed by Adams but not delivered. Stunned by Adams's naked attempt to pack the judiciary with Federalists, Jefferson attempted to block the appointments by withholding the commissions. Jefferson instructed Secretary of State James Madison not to deliver the papers to the judges. Several of the would-be appointees, one of them named William Marbury, took their case to the Supreme Court by suing the Secretary of State.

Marbury v. *Madison* was a landmark decision in the history of the U.S. judiciary. Chief Justice John Marshall, a Federalist appointed by Adams, ruled that it was unconstitutional for Jefferson or Madison to deny Marbury's appointment. Perhaps most importantly, the case served to establish what in legal terms is today called judicial review—the right of the Supreme Court to declare a law of Congress unconstitutional. This would become an essential working part of the American system of checks and balances.

Chief Justice Marshall wrote in the Court's decision, "it is emphatically the province and duty of the judicial department to say what the law is." But he went on to say that the law that allegedly enabled Marbury to bring suit (the Judicial Act of 1789) was itself unconstitutional, so the midnight judges never received their appointments. In the end, Jefferson prevailed.

Another immediate concern Jefferson had as the newly elected president was the desire of Americans to settle the vast American west—in particular, a stretch of territory called Louisiana. Although it had once been a part of the French empire, since 1763 the land had belonged to Spain. Then Spain gave Louisiana back to France. The French general Napoleon Bonaparte, who had come to power in a coup in 1799, not only wanted to expand his own empire but also to prevent further expansion of the United States. The acquisition of Louisiana from Spain, he believed, would be a way to accomplish both goals.

"Every eye in the U.S. is now fixed on this affair of Louisiana. Perhaps nothing since the revolutionary war has produced more uneasy sensations through the body of the nation," Jefferson wrote in 1802. At that time the Louisiana Territory was wild and unsettled. Roving Indian tribes, trappers, and traders were virtually its sole inhabitants. It comprised the western half of the Mississippi River basin, from the modern state of Louisiana north to Minnesota and west to the Rocky Mountains, approximately 828,000 square miles in all. Jefferson knew that the Louisiana Territory, with its great natural resources, was valuable and that U.S. access to those resources should not be limited by foreign powers.

Concerned about the French taking control of the Mississippi River and its outlet, New Orleans, Jefferson sent an envoy, John Livingston, and later James Monroe, to France in hopes of persuading Napoleon not to take the territory, or at least to negotiate the privilege of access to New Orleans for U.S. sailing

87

ships. The passage of goods through New Orleans was crucial for the success of America's foreign trade. Jefferson even secured funds from Congress to use as leverage in the negotiations. Jefferson wrote to Monroe, "The future destinies of our country hang on the event of this negotiation."

By the time Monroe reached Paris, however, Napoleon had lost interest in his New World expansion project. He was preoccupied with his conquests in Europe and the possibility of war with Britain. Also Napoleon had experienced numerous setbacks in his quest for power, including an outbreak of yellow fever that had wiped out a good portion of his army. What he was now interested in was money. When the American negotiators offered to buy New Orleans from Napoleon, he offered to sell the United States the entire territory. That way he would not only add needed cash to his treasury but also he thought he would gain an ally in his ongoing wars with Great Britain.

In May 1803, the Louisiana Purchase, which in effect doubled the size of the United States and brought both the Missouri and Mississippi Rivers within its borders, was complete. The final selling price was $15,000,000, only slightly more than the price Jefferson had been willing to pay for New Orleans alone.

The Louisiana Purchase Treaty was ratified by Congress on October 20, 1803, by a vote of 24 to 7 in an almost entirely partisan vote. All but one Federalist voted against the treaty's ratification, which the Republicans and the American people supported overwhelmingly.

Federalists protested that Jefferson did not have the power to buy the land. They argued that the Constitution did not grant the president the authority to use Congressional funds for real estate deals. Some accused Jefferson of being politically motivated, of buying the land simply in order to add Republican states to the Union. Still others wondered what had actually been purchased. Definite borders had not been entirely established, and the land was, for the most part, unexplored. However the romantic notion of expansion and discovery appealed to the idealistic and curious American public, which supported Jefferson's interest in acquiring the western lands.

Jefferson set out to discover more about the expansive new territory. He had planned to send an expedition to explore Louisiana for some time. He had even requested permission to do so from the Spanish minister in Washington and approached Congress for funding for the exploration. Now that the territory belonged to the United States, it was important that the land be surveyed in order to show that its purchase was truly a bargain for the United States. No doubt Jefferson was looking to silence his Federalist critics.

If an expedition could discover a route to the Pacific it would open up new areas for U.S. fur traders. But Jefferson's most compelling reason for sending the expedition was to acquire knowledge of the territory's wildlife, vegetation, and climate, and to become acquainted with the American Indians that inhabited the vast area.

In 1803 Jefferson asked his private secretary, Meriwether Lewis, a former army captain with some knowledge of the western territory, to lead the first Louisiana expedition. Captain William Clark joined the party as coleader. Their plan was to ascend the Missouri River to its source, cross the Rocky Mountains, and descend the Columbia River to its mouth. Jefferson instructed the two explorers to produce an accurate map of the country they covered, to note its terrain and its resources, and to document the living habits of the Indians they encountered along the way. Jefferson told Lewis to prepare for the expedition by studying astronomy, surveying, botany, and biology with the prominent American scientists of the day.

Congress approved Jefferson's request for funding, and on May 14, 1804, Lewis and Clark, carrying Jefferson's detailed instructions, led their team of explorers from St. Louis into the wild unknown, beginning an arduous journey that would last more than two years and that would entail incredible hardships.

Though a few skeptics criticized the Lewis and Clark expedition as folly and a waste of money, generally the American public strongly supported Jefferson's decision to explore the Louisiana Territory and to chart the westward expansion of the new nation. The commercial and scientific possibilities alone seemed sufficient to justify the exploration, and a certain degree of curiosity lurked in the mind of all Americans.

The Louisiana Purchase Treaty and the start of the Lewis and Clark expedition served as a fitting finale to what had been a very successful first term for President Jefferson. But 1804 was an election year, and Jefferson had to decide whether he wanted to continue in public office. He believed, as did most Republicans, that he had the support of the American people for another term. But he still yearned to return to private life, Monticello, and his beloved Albemarle County. The Republican party, however, would not take "no" for an answer. Republican Congressmen convened and voted unanimously to renominate Jefferson for president.

This time Aaron Burr was not nominated as Jefferson's running mate. During Jefferson's first term, Burr had not impressed the president with his abilities and had lost favor with many people in the Republican Party. Seeing his political career disintegrate, Burr challenged his longtime political enemy, Alexander Hamilton, the leader of the Federalists, to a duel. Although he was against dueling, Hamilton believed that not to accept Burr's challenge would mark him as a coward and ruin his political career. He accepted.

In January of that year Jefferson's sister Mary had died, and in April his daughter Maria passed away following a very difficult childbirth. With the sudden loss of his oldest sister and his daughter, Jefferson once more felt the grief he had felt when his wife Martha had died 22 years earlier. There was more death to come.

Shortly before dawn on July 11, 1804, Hamilton, his "second" or assistant, Nathaniel Pendleton, and his personal physician climbed into a small rowboat and set off on a three-mile trip across the Hudson River from New York City to Weehawken, New Jersey, where the duel was scheduled to take place. Aaron Burr and his second, William P. Van Ness, had already arrived when Hamilton and his party came ashore.

In those days gentlemen occasionally chose to settle their differences by means of a duel, and duels were always conducted according to a strict, centuries-old code of etiquette. The "seconds"—men who were usually close personal friends of the men fighting the duel—assisted the duelists.

Once formal greetings were exchanged, the two seconds drew lots to determine where each duelist would stand and which second would explain the rules of the duel. When the drawing of lots was finished, Pendleton had won. He proceeded to explain that the two duelists, pistols in hand, would stand on their designated spots, which were marked exactly 10 yards apart. Then Pendleton explained that he would call out the command for the two men to raise their weapons, aim, and fire.

Burr and Hamilton assumed their positions, and Pendleton repeated his explanation of the rules of the duel. Both men were visibly nervous and perspiring freely. It was a hot, humid summer morning, and each was contemplating the possibility of his impending death. As Pendleton spoke, the duelists practiced raising and lowering their pistols. Hamilton paused to put his glasses on, commented on the glare the morning sun was creating, and apologized for the delay. That someone about to open fire on another would so remember his manners is a comment on the man, his times, and the art of dueling.

In fact, Hamilton had decided weeks before that he would not try to kill Burr in the duel, that he would either miss intentionally or not fire at all. He had spent the days leading up to the duel writing a will and farewell letters to close friends. He had not told his wife, Elizabeth, about the duel, but he spent the evening of July 10 composing a last letter to her. He ended it by saying, "Adieu best of wives and best of women, embrace all my children for me."

When Pendleton cried out "Present!" Hamilton

and Burr raised their weapons and took aim. Burr fired first, and Hamilton's pistol went off almost at the same time as he fell. Burr's bullet hit Hamilton squarely and shattered his spine. The Federalist leader died some 30 hours later at his home.

There followed an impressive outpouring of national grief. Although Burr had won the duel, he had killed one of the most brilliant men in America. As a result he alienated himself even further from members of both the Republican and the Federalist parties. His political career had been ended forever. Consequently, not Burr but the popular New York governor George Clinton became Jefferson's new running mate.

Less than a month after Burr's duel with Hamilton, it became apparent that Burr was not only a vainglorious fool but a liar and a traitor as well. Evidence surfaced that he had conspired with foreign governments to undermine the U.S. government and divide the United States territorially through military force. He was eventually tried for treason. Though his guilt was not sufficiently proven before Justice John Marshall, who used a bit of legal trickery to avoid conviction, Burr was never able to salvage his political career. He ran off to Europe, devised numerous other schemes to overthrow the U.S. government from abroad, and eventually returned to New York, where for a while he practiced law. He married, divorced, and died a very lonely man.

Though Jefferson was deeply troubled by Hamilton's death and the scandals that pursued Aaron Burr, his second run for the presidency got off to an excellent start. As the 1804 campaign season began, Jefferson wrote to Monroe that he felt sure of winning all but four states. As it turned out, Jefferson had underestimated his own popularity. He won the election by a landslide, carrying all but two states and receiving 162 electoral votes. His Federalist opponent, Charles Cotesworth Pinckney, in a very poor showing, received only 14 electoral votes.

Jefferson took the oath of office and began his second term as president of the United States in March 1805. In his inaugural address he thanked his countrymen for their confidence in him. He declared that he himself believed that during his first term he had lived up to the high standards he had set for himself, as well as the principles on which the new nation had been founded. He underscored the many accomplishments of his first term, including the improved fiscal state of the nation. He also expressed concern over the plight of "the aboriginal inhabitants" of the country, the native American Indians, who were facing extinction at the hands of the European settlers.

One of the first successes of Jefferson's second term as president was a project that had begun during his first term— the Lewis and Clark expedition to explore the American west. News had been so long in coming that many had given up the explorers for dead. Jefferson himself, almost always the optimist, had even begun to fear the worst. After two long years of waiting, though, Jefferson finally received word from the Lewis and Clark expedition in 1805. He was overjoyed.

Lewis and Clark had endured disease, hunger, and exposure to brutally harsh weather. They had forged rivers, crossed the great plains, and climbed the Rocky Mountains. They had encountered wild and often dangerous animals, and had lost their way numerous times. But the two men had returned, alive and with a wealth of information.

At the house at Monticello, Jefferson displayed many of the Indian artifacts that Lewis and Clark had acquired during their expedition. The explorers had even sent back a living magpie and a prairie dog, which Jefferson donated to a Philadelphia museum. He also planted some of the assorted seeds the explorers had brought from the west. For Jefferson, the courage of Lewis and Clark and their team of brave explorers was the very same courage that had enabled the colonies to gain their independence and to forge a new nation. He was proud to have been a part of it.

Early in his second term as president, Jefferson sat for America's renowned portrait painter Gilbert Stuart. But soon Jefferson had little time for such indulgences. He became increasingly involved in European affairs.

Britain still didn't respect the idea that the United States of America was a sovereign, independent country. The British Navy began interfering with American ships on the high seas. They even boarded American ships and apprehended sailors whom they claimed were actually deserters from the British Navy. The practice was known as impressment. Federalists criticized Jefferson's administration for not taking action to protect American vessels from European abuses, particularly the impressment of American sailors.

In June 1807, the British frigate *Leopard* fired on the American naval ship *Chesapeake* about 10 miles off the coast of Norfolk, Virginia, killing 4 Americans, injuring 18. The British apprehended 3 so-called desert-

The Bettmann Archive

Then Lewis and Clark returned from their famous expedition, Thomas Jefferson displayed many of the animal trophies and Indian artifacts which they brought back in the hallway of Monticello. Over the door is the unusual clock which Jefferson invented. From the horizontal slats on the walls on either side, and the placement of the round weights, he could tell immediately what day it was, as well as the time.

ers. The British commander justified the action by saying that the U.S. Navy was harboring British traitors.

For most Americans, whether the men in question were actually deserters or not was not really the issue. The attack on the American ship was an act of war, calling for retaliatory measures. Federalist criticism of Jefferson's failure to act grew louder. Republicans, too, were outraged and called for drastic action. At public meetings throughout the country, the outcry was for revenge.

Jefferson remained calm and followed a moderate course. He realized that the country was not prepared for a war with Britain, especially financially. In any case, he preferred to seek a peaceful solution. He demanded that the four alleged traitors be returned to the United States and that the British apologize for the attack, pay for the damage they had caused, and discontinue any further harassment of American ships. While the British were considering these demands, Jefferson moved to strengthen the nation's armed forces, just in case the country had to go to war.

The British refused to meet Jefferson's demands and indicated they had every intention of continuing the practice of impressment of sailors whom they thought were British deserters. France was also interfering with American shipping. Jefferson told the Congress that he recognized "the great and increasing dangers with which our vessels, our seamen, and merchandise, are threatened on the high seas and elsewhere, from the belligerent powers of Europe." He recommended a piece of legislation, called the

Embargo Act of 1807, that would cut off U.S. trade with both countries.

To Jefferson's dismay, the British and French proved less dependent on American trade than he thought they were. The Embargo Act backfired on American merchants, who relied heavily on trade with Europe. The legislation was an embarrassment for Jefferson that plagued him through the final year of his second term.

Though the failure of the Embargo Act hung like a dark cloud over Jefferson's administration, the president continued to enjoy great popular support. So much so, in fact, that Republicans urged him to seek re-election in 1808. But this time Jefferson would not run. He believed that no president should serve more than two terms. Remembering the wisdom of George Washington, Jefferson said, "I should unwillingly be the person who, disregarding the sound precedent set by an illustrious predecessor, should furnish the first example of prolongation beyond the second term of office."

As his final days as president counted down, Jefferson eagerly anticipated his return to Monticello. He wrote to his old friend James Monroe that he longed to go back "to a scene of tranquillity, amidst my family and friends, more congenial to my age and natural inclinations." During those days Jefferson also wrote, "Within a few days I retire to my family, my books and farms . . . Never did a prisoner, released from his chains, feel such relief as I shall on shaking off the shackles of power."

8

The Retiring Statesman

ON MARCH 4, 1809, Jefferson and his grandson Thomas Jefferson Randolph rode up Pennsylvania Avenue to the Capitol to attend the inauguration of Thomas Jefferson's old friend James Madison, who on that day became the fourth president of the United States.

Jefferson, the retiring president, was pleased to have such a worthy successor, and it showed in the satisfied expression on his face. As he watched Chief Justice Marshall administer the oath of office to Madison, Jefferson must have recalled the two times he too had stood before the American people and had sworn to carry out the duties of the presidency to the best of his ability. Looking back he was surely satisfied with his many great accomplishments as a member of Congress, as governor of Virginia, as secretary of state, as vice-president, and as the nation's chief executive.

He had taken measures to pay the national debt, strengthened the national defense, and secured a balanced judiciary. He had asserted America's right to free trade and use of the high seas while successfully keeping the country out of war. He had expanded America's borders beyond the Mississippi River. And he had fought for states' rights while establishing a strong central government. Most importantly, he had inspired a revolution based on democratic ideals.

When Madison finished delivering his inaugural address, Jefferson and other well-wishers attended a reception at the Madison home and later that evening the presidential inaugural ball. Many said their last farewells to the retiring president. All were saddened by his impending departure. Jefferson left Washington, D.C., on March 11, having sent wagons filled with his belongings ahead of him.

The journey was a difficult one. He travelled eight hours in a snowstorm, and, though now 65 years old, he abandoned his coach because of treacherous road conditions and travelled three days on horseback. Finally he arrived in Monticello on March 15.

Over the years Monticello has been preserved much as it was when Jefferson returned there in 1809 to begin his retirement. Approaching Jefferson's house, one is struck by the apparent simplicity of its design and its gentle curves. Jefferson's love for French architecture is evident in its structure and layout. For instance Jefferson designed a single-story house in the style of the French country manor home, rather than a house with many levels. Also like the French estates, Monticello is a relatively small house nestled in a peaceful wooded setting atop a hill.

Walking through the porticoed entrance at Monticello, one stands in a bright, spacious welcoming room. Inside, above the large wooden doors, is a unique calendar clock, which Jefferson designed himself. It is run by cannonball-like weights that move slowly down the wall as the hours go by. The days of the week are marked off on the wall so that one need only observe the position of the weights to find out what day it is. The weights have to be pulled back up by hand at regular intervals. A copper gong on the roof sounds on the hour.

Also in this welcoming room are exhibited an assortment of fascinating artifacts that Jefferson collected during his lifetime or received as gifts. In fact Monticello is in some ways more like a museum of art and natural history than a private residence. Immediately upon entering the house, on either side of the room are Indian relics brought back from the Lewis and Clark expedition—mastodon bones and tusks, antlers of American moose, elk, and deer. Mounted on the wall is a huge buffalo head from the western plains of the United States. Also on display are various samples of minerals, sea shells, and other specimens of nature from all over the world.

The library at Monticello, which houses an extensive collection of books and maps, reflects the great value Jefferson placed on learning. The subjects of history, literature, science, architecture, and exploration are all well represented on his shelves, where volumes are carefully arranged by subject.

Jefferson's love for art is also apparent in the wide-ranging collection of painting and sculpture at Monticello. In the parlor alone there are more than 40 paintings, many of which he brought back from Europe. Also, Jefferson brought from Paris many fine furnishings that grace the rooms at Monticello, such as a marble clock, several mahogany chairs, and enormous ceiling-to-floor mirrors. Houdon's bust of Voltaire is prominently displayed in Monticello's receiving room.

Throughout the house are many of Jefferson's fascinating inventions, for the most part designed for the efficient and economical running of his household, and the speedy conduct of his personal and professional affairs. In his study is a swivel chair and a revolving table that allowed Jefferson access to numerous papers and books without his ever moving from his seat.

On the table is one invention that always fascinates visitors—Jefferson's polygraph. Though extremely primitive by today's standards, Jefferson's ingenious polygraph allowed him to make an exact copy of a letter, document, or drawing. Jefferson designed the device so that when he wrote or drew with one pen, another pen simultaneously moved on a separate page, making a flawless duplicate. Jefferson's telescope is also there on display for visitors to see.

For years Jefferson's daughter Martha and her family lived at Edgehill, an estate only a few miles east of Monticello. They moved back to Monticello soon after the former president's return home in 1809. By now Martha had eight children. The oldest, Anne Cary, was recently married, and the oldest boy, Thomas, was attending school in Philadelphia. Martha still had six children under her care, and by 1818 would add three more to the fold. Jefferson, who for years had spoken of a peaceful retirement at Monticello, now found himself in the company of six children, all under the age of 13. As always, he rose to the occasion, playing the role of grandfather with vigor and tenderness.

The Bettmann Archive

During Thomas Jefferson's second term as president, he was preoccupied with the issue of impressment. British naval officers frequently boarded American ships and seized sailors who were then accused of being deserters from the British navy. Impressment was contrary to international law—much like the taking of American hostages in Iran and Lebanon today.

In his retirement Jefferson indulged in many old and new projects. One new project was the building of a small house on a site he called Poplar Forest. Now that Monticello was bustling with children, Jefferson built the house at Poplar Forest so that he would have a place to be alone for days at a time to write and reflect. Poplar Forest was about 90 miles from Monticello in Bedford County, but Jefferson made the trip frequently despite the distance.

Though at one point he broke his wrist falling down a few stairs, he continued to write and plant. He even found time to try his hand at milling grain and manufacturing cloth. Never entirely satisfied with Monticello, Jefferson also spent hours pouring over plans for the construction of additional rooms and gardens for the estate.

One of the brightest and most satisfying aspects of Jefferson's retirement was his reconciliation with his old friend John Adams. After the election of 1800, Adams had returned to Massachusetts bitter and defeated. Jefferson had been angered by Adams's appointment of the "midnight judges," which he viewed as a sour attempt to hinder his Republican administration.

For more than a decade it seemed that their relationship had ended. However a short letter from Adams to Jefferson in 1811 prompted the two to resume their friendship. The correspondence began what would become one of the richest literary exchanges in American history. In their letters to each other, the two former presidents reflected on their past experiences as well as on current developments. Their subject matter knew no bounds—politics, economics, history, philosophy, religion, and science.

Letters continued to pass between them right up until the end of their lives.

Jefferson continued to follow politics from his hill-top estate. He was especially troubled by the War of 1812, when the American Army invaded British North America—what is now known as Canada. Jefferson watched with compassion as his friend President Madison struggled to achieve peace with Britain. When the British and Canadians invaded Washington, D.C., destroying many of the city's public buildings, Jefferson was deeply saddened, particularly when the Library of Congress was burned. He condemned the British for committing "acts of barbarism which do not belong to a civilized age"—forgetting perhaps that the attack on Washington had been in retaliation for the destruction of York (modern day Toronto) by the American Army.

Jefferson offered to sell Congress nearly 6,500 volumes from his own collection of books, which had been purchased in bookstores and from private individuals in countries throughout the world. After some deliberation, Congress paid $23,950 for 6,487 books from Jefferson's library. These books became the basis of the Congressional library we know today, and many of them can still be read there today.

Unable to look at empty shelves in his own home, Jefferson began to rebuild his book collection. Jefferson's lifelong commitment to education never faded, even during his final years. During the early years of American independence, his plan for a state educational system was rejected in Virginia. Still, he insisted that no republic could remain strong without a commitment to education, from the lower grades through to university level, for all its people.

During his years as president, Jefferson once more called for a "university on a plan so broad and liberal and modern, as to be worth patronizing with the public support." He made blueprints for its buildings, proposed a complete curriculum, specified the professors to be recruited, outlined various means of financing the institution, and even picked what he considered to be the ideal site—Charlottesville.

During his retirement Jefferson continued his efforts to establish the university. In 1816 the Virginia state legislature passed a bill drafted by Jefferson creating Central College, which Jefferson hoped would become the University of Virginia. Within three years, his dream became reality. The University of Virginia, one of the first state universities in the country, was born.

Jefferson directed all of the designing and construction of the new university. He hired skilled stone masons and carpenters, selected many of the building materials himself, and continued to seek financial support for the school. Not surprisingly, Jefferson gave special attention to the building of the library. He designed it after the famous Pantheon, an ancient building in Rome, and filled it with a wealth of scholarly books and materials. He drafted by-laws, rules for student conduct, degree requirements, and oversaw countless other details of the new university.

Jefferson made the University of Virginia the most liberal institution of learning in the world. There were no religious tests or practices, the curriculum was entirely elective, the professors were equals in departments headed by rotating chairmen whom they elected, and an honor system guided student life and discipline. Thus Jefferson created an educational model that would be followed by many of the world's finest institutions of higher learning.

In 1824, Jefferson received a distinguished visitor from France, the Marquis de Lafayette, who had helped General Washington fight the American Revolution. A special dinner in his honor was served in the large, circular room of the Rotunda at the University of Virginia in Charlottesville. During the course of the meal, the former president was toasted as the founder of the university. Later he gave what would be his last public address, reaffirming the great love he had for his country and his sincere hopes for its prosperous future.

A short time after the opening of the university, Jefferson wrote of the future generations of students that would pass through it, "I hope its influence on their virtue, freedom, fame, and happiness, will be salutary and permanent." Jefferson regarded the founding of the University of Virginia as one of the greatest accomplishments of his life. Indeed, the school would shape the minds of many students for generations.

The university's doors were opened to students in March 1825. In the years that followed, Jefferson continued to be involved in the school's administration, despite failing health.

Surrounded by his grandchildren at Monticello, Jefferson realized that the future now belonged to them, that his own life's energy was waning. He wrote his last will and testament in March 1826. Jefferson believed strongly in the value of education, that people should follow their instincts for learning and discovery, and that everyone must strive to use all of their talents to their fullest potential. He once wrote, "I have sworn upon the altar of God, eternal hostility against every form of tyranny over the mind of man." His hope was to impart this conviction not only to his grandchildren but to countless generations of Americans to come after them.

Jefferson was invited to Washington, D.C. on June 24, 1826 to attend ceremonies commemorating the fiftieth anniversary of the signing of the Declaration of Independence. He was forced to decline for health reasons. It was the last letter to flow from his pen. Still, recalling the days in Philadelphia a half-century earlier when he wrote the Declaration, he realized that its principles had sustained him throughout his life, and that those principles would sustain the nation in years to come. In his last letter he wrote, "All eyes are opened, or opening to the rights of man . . . Let the annual return of this day, forever refresh our recollections of those rights, and an undiminished devotion to them."

That same day Jefferson called for his doctor, Robley Dunglison, a professor of medicine at the University of Virginia. He remained at Jefferson's side and administered care as needed during his last days. On July 3, Jefferson lost consciousness but regained it for several brief moments later that day. At around 7:00 P.M. that evening he awakened and asked his doctor if it was the fourth of July. The next day, the fiftieth anniversary of the Declaration of Independence, Thomas Jefferson died. He was 83 years old.

Later that day John Adams died in Quincy, Massachusetts. A friend at Adams's bedside is said to have heard him utter his last words, "Jefferson still survives." Of course Adams was mistaken, not having heard the news of Jefferson's death. But he was not mistaken with respect to Jefferson's legacy.

That legacy is perhaps the most essential, the most far reaching, and the most enduring of any man in the history of America. As with any great philosopher, Thomas Jefferson's legacy is one of ideas. Jefferson taught his generation that government's first responsibility is to recognize and protect the rights of the individual in society. He declared that not even the government could infringe these rights, and that any government that did should be corrected, or if necessary, overthrown.

Jefferson also believed that the only just government is participatory government, that a republic is to be preferred over a monarchy. By articulating these fundamental principles with power and conviction, Jefferson gave others—on both sides of the Atlantic—the courage to struggle against their oppressors in the name of liberty and self-determination.

The phrase "Jeffersonian democracy" is often used to describe these beliefs, and in many ways they are as radical today as they were in 1776. Jeffersonian democracy endures as a model for people who wish to build free societies.

Jefferson was buried next to his wife Martha at the cemetery at Monticello. Late in his life he had designed his own tombstone. He wanted to be remembered for what he considered his three most important achievements, so he requested that it be engraved with "the following inscription, and not a word more":

Here was buried
        Thomas Jefferson
Author of the Declaration of Independence
    of the Statute of Virginia for religious freedom
    and Father of the University of Virginia.

THE DECLARATION OF INDEPENDENCE

IN CONGRESS, JULY 4, 1776
THE UNANIMOUS DECLARATION OF THE
THIRTEEN UNITED STATES OF AMERICA

When in the Course of human events, it becomes necessary for one people to dissolve the political bands which have connected them with another, and to assume among the powers of the earth, the separate and equal station to which the Laws of Nature and of Nature's God entitle them, a decent respect to the opinions of mankind requires that they should declare the causes which impel them to the separation.—We hold these truths to be self-evident, that all men are created equal, that they are endowed by their Creator with certain unalienable Rights, that among these are Life, Liberty and the pursuit of Happiness.—That to secure these rights, Governments are instituted among Men, deriving their just powers from the consent of the governed,—That whenever any Form of Government becomes destructive of these ends, it is the Right of the People to alter or to abolish it, and to institute new Government, laying its foundation on such principles and organizing its powers in such form, as to them shall seem most likely to effect their Safety and Happiness. Prudence, indeed, will dictate that Governments long established should not be changed for light and transient causes; and accordingly all experience hath shewn, that mankind are more disposed to suffer, while evils are sufferable, than to right themselves by abolishing the forms to which they are accustomed. But when a long train of abuses and usurpations, pursuing invariably the same Object evinces a design to reduce them under absolute Despotism, it is their right, it is their duty, to throw off such Government, and to provide new Guards for their future security.—Such has been the patient sufferance of these Colonies; and such is now the necessity which constrains them to alter their former Systems of Government. The history of the present King of Great Britain is a history of repeated injuries and usurpations, all having in direct object the establishment of an absolute Tyranny over these States. To prove this, let Facts be submitted to a candid world.—He has refused his Assent to Laws, the most wholesome and necessary for the public good.—He has forbidden his Governors to pass Laws of immediate and pressing importance, unless suspended in their operation till his Assent should be obtained; and when so suspended, he has utterly neglected to attend to them.—He has refused to pass other Laws for the accommodation of large districts of people, unless these people would relinquish the right of Representation in the Legislature, a right inestimable to them and formidable to tyrants only.—He has called together legislative bodies at places unusual, uncomfortable, and distant from the depository of their public Records, for the sole purpose of fatiguing them into compliance with his measures.—He has dissolved Representative Houses repeatedly, for opposing with manly firmness his invasions on the rights of the people.—He has refused for a long time, after such dissolutions, to cause others to be elected; whereby the Legislative powers, incapable of Annihilation, have returned to the People at large for their exercise; the State remaining in the mean time exposed to all the dangers of invasion from without, and convulsions within.—He has endeavoured to prevent the population of these States; for that purpose obstructing the Laws for Naturalization of Foreigners; refusing to pass others to encourage their migrations hither, and raising the conditions of new Appropriations of Lands.—He has obstructed the Administration of Justice, by refusing his Assent to Laws for establishing Judiciary powers.—He has made Judges dependent on his Will alone, for the tenure of their offices, and the amount and payment of their salaries.—He has erected a multitude of New Offices, and sent hither swarms of Officers to harass our people, and eat out their substance.—He has kept among us, in times of peace, Standing Armies without the Consent of our legislatures.—He has affected to render the Military independent of and superior to the Civil power.—He has combined with others to subject us to a jurisdiction foreign to our constitution, and unacknowledged by our laws; giving his Assent to their Acts of pretended Legislation:—For quartering large bodies of armed troops among us:— For protecting them, by a mock Trial, from punishment for any Murders which they should commit on the Inhabitants of these States:—For cutting off our Trade with all parts of the world:—For imposing Taxes on us without our Consent:—For depriving us in many cases, of the benefits of Trial by Jury:—For transporting us beyond Seas to be tried for pretended offences:—For abolishing the free System of English Laws in a neighboring Province, establishing therein an Arbitrary government, and enlarging its Boundaries so as to render it at once an example and fit instrument for introducing the same absolute rule into these Colonies:—For taking away our Charters, abolishing our most valuable Laws, and altering fundamentally the Forms of our Governments:—For suspending our own Legislatures and declaring themselves invested with power to legislate for us in all cases whatsoever.—He has abdicated Government here, by declaring us out of his Protection and waging War against us.—He has plundered our seas, ravaged our Coasts, burnt our towns, and destroyed the lives of our people.—He is at this time transporting large Armies of foreign Mercenaries to compleat the works of death, desolation and tyranny, already begun with circumstances of Cruelty & perfidy scarcely paralleled in the most barbarous ages, and totally unworthy the Head of a civilized nation.—He has constrained our fellow Citizens taken Captive on the high Seas to bear Arms against their Country, to become the executioners of their friends and Brethren, or to fall themselves by their Hands.—He has excited domestic insurrections amongst us, and has endeavoured to bring on the inhabitants of our frontiers, the merciless Indian Savages, whose known rule of warfare, is an undistinguished destruction of all ages, sexes and conditions. In every stage of these Oppressions We have Petitioned for Redress in the most humble terms: Our repeated Petitions have been answered only by repeated injury. A

Prince, whose character is thus marked by every act which may define a Tyrant, is unfit to be the ruler of a free people. Nor have We been wanting in attentions to our British brethren. We have warned them from time to time of attempts by their legislature to extend an unwarrantable jurisdiction over us. We have reminded them of the circumstances of our emigration and settlement here. We have appealed to their native justice and magnanimity, and we have conjured them by the ties of our common kindred to disavow these usurpations, which, would inevitably interrupt our connections and correspondence. They too have been deaf to the voice of justice and of consanguinity. We must, therefore, acquiesce in the necessity, which denounces our Separation, and hold them, as we hold the rest of mankind, Enemies in War, in Peace Friends.—

We, THEREFORE, the Representatives of the United States of America, in General Congress, Assembled, appealing to the Supreme Judge of the world for the rectitude of our intentions, do, in the Name, and by Authority of the good People of these Colonies, solemnly publish and declare, That these United Colonies are, and of Right ought to be FREE AND INDEPENDENT STATES; that they are Absolved from all Allegiance to the British Crown, and that all political connection between them and the State of Great Britain, is and ought to be totally dissolved; and that as Free and Independent States, they have full Power to levy War, conclude Peace, contract Alliances, establish Commerce, and to do all other Acts and Things which Independent States may of right do.—And for the support of this Declaration, with a firm reliance on the protection of divine Providence, we mutually pledge to each other our Lives, our Fortunes, and our sacred Honor.

Bibliography

Brodie, Fawn M. *Thomas Jefferson: An Intimate History*. Bantam, 1975.

Bruns, Roger. *Thomas Jefferson*. Chelsea House, 1986.

Chinard, Gilbert. *Thomas Jefferson: The Apostle of Americanism*. The University of Michigan Press, 1962.

Cunningham, Noble E., Jr. *In Pursuit of Reason: The Life of Thomas Jefferson*. Louisiana State University Press, 1987.

Dabney, Virginius. *The Jefferson Scandals: A Rebuttal*. Dodd, 1988.

Graff, Henry F. *Thomas Jefferson*. Silver Burdett, 1968.

Kimball, Marie. *Jefferson: The Road to Glory, 1743–1776*. Greenwood, 1943.

———. *Jefferson: War and Peace, 1776–1784*. Greenwood, 1947.

Malone, Dumas. *Jefferson and His Time*. (6 volumes):

———. *Jefferson the Virginian*. Little, Brown, 1948.

———. *Jefferson and the Rights of Man*. Little, Brown, 1951.

——. *Jefferson and the Ordeal of Liberty*. Little, Brown, 1962.

——. *Jefferson the President. First Term, 1801–1805*. Little, Brown, 1970.

——. *Jefferson the President. Second Term, 1805–1809*. Little, Brown, 1974.

——. *The Sage of Monticello*. Little, Brown, 1977.

Peterson, Merrill D. *Thomas Jefferson*. Penguin, 1984.

Rice, Howard C., Jr. *Thomas Jefferson's Paris*. Princeton University Press, 1976.

Stefoff, Rebecca. *Thomas Jefferson: The Third President of the United States*. Garrett, 1988.

Wills, Garry. *Inventing America: Jefferson's Declaration of Independence*. Random House, 1979.

About the Author

John W. Selfridge is an editor and free-lance writer with a special interest in twentieth-century history and culture. He received an M.A. in 1980 from Columbia University, where he studied literature and philosophy, and he is currently enrolled at Rutgers University Law School. An editor for a major New York City publishing house, he has been consulted on more than 100 young adult biographies. He is the author of *John F. Kennedy: Courage in Crisis* and *Franklin D. Roosevelt: The People's President* in the Great Lives Series.

died 4 July 1826